BUILDING RESULTS

The Ultimate How-To Guide
For New Home Sales

Robert E. Hafer, MIRM, CSP

Foreword by Karen Taylor

Upper Canyon Road Publishing House
Richardson, Texas
2006

Upper Canyon Road Publishing House
914 Chadwick Drive † Richardson, Texas 75080

Printed in the United States of America
Distributed by Upper Canyon Road Publishing
Printed by Executive Press, www.executivepress.com
Cover design by Kem Ormand

ISBN 0-9786587-0-1

Seminars and workshops by Robert E. Hafer may be scheduled through
Robert E. Hafer & Associates LLC
4361 Mill Creek Road, Dallas, TX 75244
972-795-5926 † 972-239-1808
buildingresults@BobHafer.com

Building Results

**The Ultimate How-To Guide
For New Home Sales**

To my wife Donna –

For her continuing love,
support and encouragement.

Contents

Foreword

The first time I heard Bob Hafer's voice on the telephone, I was struck by the rich sincerity of his words. He was a man on a mission, and that mission came through loud and clear. He had a message to give to the new home sales community – an audience he had targeted for most of his successful career.

I was instantly enchanted. As a writer, journalist, editor and ghost writer for the past 36 years, I've probably interviewed close to 1,000 people, and I've learned to make almost instant assessments of personalities. Naturally, I don't hit the nail on the head 100 percent of the time, but I am right more often than not.

My assistant, Will Ward, and I met Bob at his office in Addison, Texas, a booming suburb of Dallas. It was a typical hot, summer day in Dallas, I was on a cane as a result of ongoing knee problems, Will was a little rumpled and hot, and Bob was cool and crisp as a cucumber.

The next two hours flew by as Bob enthusiastically explained his project. He felt that he was on the threshold of a new phase of his life. In his late 50s, as dynamic as a 30-year-old, and as focused as a Patriot missile, he was almost intimidating in his intensity. Bottom line – he wanted someone to edit his book, *Building Results*. It seemed like a no-brainer. He had accumulated literally pounds of paperwork in several loose-leaf notebooks that he used as workbooks, training guides and chapters for his forthcoming book. There really wasn't much interviewing to be done – it looked as if it would be a research and organizational task, assembling his rough draft into a readable, effective book.

Bob Hafer is a well-known name in Dallas homebuilder circles and has served in several capacities for the Home Builders Association of Greater Dallas. At the time I had about 20 years' experience with the HBA and currently served on their communication committee. My public relations firm had been agency of record for two HBA Parades and for the association itself. We seemed to be perfectly matched to achieve his publishing goal.

I nosed around several members of HBA to see what they thought of this potential new client and his ambitious goals. Results were positive, and Will and I congratulated ourselves on landing an interesting piece of business – a retainer for a six-month period that would result in an excellent guide for new home salespeople.

Best of all, this was the kind of work I loved – editing something new, different and creative that would have a positive impact on the reader.

It took several months for us to get a real grip on the materials – in part because we actually had too much material. We were overwhelmed by the vast amount of information. In hindsight we should have taken one set of training materials and given the rest back to Bob. But as we all know, hindsight has 20/20 vision.

One year later, I was still working on our first draft, with all expectations of the work proceeding into September 2005. In my experience, the book should have been completed within the six-month allotment. However, reality bites, and as I write this, I actually can see the light at the end of the tunnel. Continued organization, additional information and bold editing of existing chapters contributed to a bumpy, but educational, process.

And a most remarkable occurrence – I came to believe that Bob has developed something that truly is unique to the new home building industry. The information he has gathered and the process he has developed leaves me awestruck. Within a few pages in a book that probably can be read over a weekend he introduces a concept so simple and yet so powerful that I am adopting it for my own work. I eagerly anticipate the day when I will sit at the back of a room; watching his book sell to an enthusiastic audience and listening to Bob give an overview of *Building Results*.

Congratulations – regardless of how you have come to be reading this, whether as a find at the bookstore, a gift from a friend, part of a training program or found on the seat of a bus – you are in for the ride of your life.

And if you understand what you're reading, truly grasp Bob's concept and employ it in your daily work, I guarantee you will succeed in sales as you never have before. If you don't, well, Bob will give you your money back.

I promise this: You simply cannot fail to increase your current sales of new homes if you carefully follow Bob's magnificent theory.

Karen Taylor
Dallas, Texas
February 2006

Chapter 1

Turning Point

    The great epiphany of my sales career – one that I hope will become the magnificent turning point in your successful career – came at a sales meeting for one of the biggest volume home builders in the nation. I witnessed the most blatant display of apathy I've ever seen in my business life.

    As the regional sales and marketing director for one of the nation's largest residential home builders' mid-Atlantic region, my responsibilities included oversight of sales training for ten divisions with seventy salespeople managing more than one hundred model homes in five states.

    Once each quarter the company's corporate office sponsored a one-day sales training seminar conducted by some of the homebuilding industry's top trainers as well as nationally known sales motivators and trainers. These well-known names in inspirational teaching were retained to conduct home-selling seminars designed to jump-start the careers of newly hired salespeople.

    That life-changing day, Brian Tracey, a highly respected authority on personal and business success, led the seminar I attended. At the time, Brian's portfolio was amazing – more than 2,000 seminars for more than 500 companies. He remains one of the biggest stars in sales training and personal motivation.

    I was shocked at the low turnout - only twenty-eight of seventy salespeople chose to attend. When I questioned people about the dismal attendance, the answer was equally surprising. *"The training is optional,"* one salesperson told me. *"If the salespeople have more pressing business, they just skip it."*

    Frankly, I couldn't believe it. Why anyone would choose not to take advantage of an opportunity to learn selling skills from of one of the nation's top trainers? Was it possible these salespeople saw no benefit in training and felt that handling day-to-day business was more important? If this was true, then did it make fiscal and strategic sense for my home builder company – which like all companies is very focused on the bottom line - to continue sponsoring these expensive seminars?

Hoping for answers, and knowing this was information that could make or break the success of the training program, I visited my company's corporate training director. Judging from the look on his face, he was as surprised and concerned as I was. We talked about solutions for encouraging participation. Several good ideas were developed, but I still felt something was missing.

It was as if a large black hole had appeared in my experience as well as my company's formidable reputation for developing top salespeople. As I was preparing to leave, the training director suggested I audit the next corporate sales training seminar.

The builder was Ryland Homes – known as one of the sharpest, most profit-oriented new home builders in America. The firm had developed an excellent training program featuring some of the most dynamic names in the business – the late Dave Stone, Tom Richey, and the local president of Dale Carnegie. The program lasted five days and focused on teaching the widely accepted new home critical path sales method. I agreed to attend the course and volunteered to work with and coach salespeople if the occasion arose.

Twenty-six people attended the five-day program. Each instructor did an outstanding job communicating how to sell new homes. They taught how to greet, qualify, demonstrate the home and home site, how to overcome objections and close. I was impressed. Surely salespeople would return to their model homes and begin selling new homes aggressively.

Following the seminar each salesperson was 'mystery shopped' to ensure that their new selling skills were being used. I made arrangements with the corporate training director to receive copies of all twenty-six reports. I began reading and listening to the audiotapes, which averaged one to two hours. It took a month to complete these, transcribe the tapes, complete the hand-written reports and mail copies to Ryland's training director.

The distressful conclusion? Skills taught in the five-day seminar were not consistently used by the majority of the sales staff.

I was completely stumped. What caused these salespeople to abandon what were clearly success-generating skills taught by the best new home sales experts in the nation?

I phoned each person directly to ask why they chose not to use the skills taught during the seminar. Over and over I heard: *"What we were taught doesn't work in the real world. The selling techniques and methods sound good, but they are more theoretical than practical"* and *"Customers have their own buying agendas"*.

The shocking fact was that the critical path designed by builders for their salespersons and the reality of the buyer process were completely opposite. No wonder the salespeople weren't receptive and the process – which sounded great in theory – was sadly lacking in reality.

Critical Path Sales Method

When I questioned the salespeople, their answers were almost identical. *"The critical path sales process does not align with my customers' agenda."*

I asked for specific examples. Here's a typical response: *"When customers visit model homes they first want to look and get a feel for the home before they answer questions. But the critical path method instructs the salesperson to ask a series of qualifying questions before a customer is allowed to tour the models. Asking qualifying questions before a customer has time to look and experience the model home sets up an adversarial relationship that pits the sales process against the customers' buying process."*

It made sense. When I asked myself how I like to buy, I realized I prefer to be left alone until I have questions that need answers. That was my turning point moment. Could it be that controlling customers might not be in the best interest of salespeople?

My belief system was seriously challenged. I knew there had to be a way for both salesperson and customer to achieve individual goals. The salesperson wants to sell a home and the buyer wants to buy a home. What could be done to satisfy these goals without sacrificing all the good things critical path selling offers? And was critical path selling even the best route to take? As a long-time, new home sales professional, my belief system was being seriously questioned.

For the next year, I remained actively involved in Ryland's corporate training program. I continued to listen to mystery shops and question each salesperson about the results of his or her shop. The answers I got took on a familiar tone, *"Customers don't want to be controlled"*.

Meeting Customer Needs

Soon after, I took over the position of Ryland's sales training director and began to make sweeping changes in the training course.

1. Class sizes were reduced from twenty-six to sixteen.

2. The sixteen participants were separated into four groups of four people.

3. Ryland sales managers were invited to participate as coaches for each group.

4. Role-play sessions after each lecture helped participants immediately practice what they were learning.

5. Videotape sessions were added to demonstrate the skills of critical path selling.

6. Mystery shopping followed each seminar's completion.

The course was better, but I still had the feeling that the sales process we were teaching didn't meet the customer's needs. I was now seriously questioning the benefits of critical path selling. A revolutionary concept had begun to evolve: was critical path selling all about doing things to customers but not doing things for customers?

A breakthrough completely changed my thinking and provided a way to meet the needs of both the salesperson and customer. Some of Ryland's veteran salespeople who had attended the company's critical path training wanted to add a second class that would take them to the next level of selling. They felt they understood critical path selling, and they wanted additional training that would help them better communicate with their customers.

Chapter 2

Communication Principles and New Home Selling

To satisfy the needs of the salespeople and myself, I began to interview industry experts as well as a carefully chosen group outside the industry. This led me to the doorstep of John LaValle, president of NLP Seminars Group International. NLP, the acronym for Neuro-Linguistics Programming, was the basis of John's concept of successful selling.

NLP uses very intense psychology to understand human behavior and interactions. Some of the concepts can be complex, but others are amazingly simple. John and I both felt that NLP could help Ryland's salespeople become better communicators. He was retained to develop a selling skills class using the rapport building techniques of NLP.

With John's help and a 13-weekend course on NLP, I discovered how to bridge the needs of the customer with the needs of the salesperson. This discovery helped me to understand what may be the most important information a sales person can learn and use:

1. New home selling is intelligent conversation between two parties who have a similar goal in mind – the purchase and sale of a new home.

2. This goal is accomplished only when a salesperson and prospect discover common points of interest that brings about alignment and agreement.

3. These two critical issues require a simple formula – in order to lead, a salesperson first must be willing to follow.

The first two concepts were easy to understand but the third concept of following was hard to accept because all my previous training stressed the need to control the customer through qualifying questions. Successfully employing these ideas required rethinking years of traditional new home sales training.

John's training and the NLP rapport building concepts taught me that the questions traditionally asked of home buyers were putting the salesperson and customer at odds with each other. The relationship was out of balance, probably the worst thing that can happen in the context of a sales process.

I began to understand that successful new home selling is the result of excellent communication skills, not a critical path selling process. My task was becoming clear: understand how people communicate with each other and learn what communication skills work best in most interpersonal situations.

My goal with this book is to help you take a more direct path to that knowledge and the unlimited success to which it can lead. In truth, these skills are useful not only for your sales work but for almost every interpersonal relationship in your life.

The following condenses the primary factors of NLP as they apply to sales. These six communication principles follow some of the tenets of NLP rapport building, acknowledge the needs of customers and enable salespeople to meet those needs while balancing their selling priorities. The six communication principles are as follows:

1. You are always communicating.

2. The mind and body are parts of the same system.

3. Ride the horse in the direction it is going.

4. The person with the most knowledge will have the most influence.

5. The map is not the territory.

6. The exception is not the rule.

These six communication principles represent the foundation of *Building Results*. Read each principle carefully, pausing to consider how that concept positively affects your relationship with your customers. I suggest you read this chapter repeatedly – perhaps every morning before you begin your sales day.

Then, I want you to consider actual selling situations where the outcome might have been different if you had followed the ideas inherent in the six communication principles.

Please keep your mind open to all the wonderful possibilities these ideas afford you in your selling career and your personal day-to-day life as you interact with family, friends, customers, and business acquaintances.

You Are Always Communicating

You constantly communicate with others with a variety of methods – the car you drive, the home you purchase, your clothing, your friends, your vocabulary – right down to the smile you present when you meet someone for the first time.

Every word, every action, every decision you make, every facial expression, even the rate, pace, pitch and tone of your voice communicates who you are and how you think.

Keep in mind: the words you choose communicate your level of education; your facial expression and body language communicate your state of mind; your tonality communicates your sincerity. You may be sure this constant state of communications helps your customers form impressions based on what they see, hear and feel.

The following chart illustrates by percentage how your physiology, tonality and words impact your ability to establish rapport with another person.

Communication Element	% of Impact on Rapport
Physiology	55%
Tonality	38%
Words	7%

Physiology

Your physiology accounts for 55% of impact on rapport. More than half of your ability to achieve agreement and alignment with a customer is connected to physiology – how you position, express and carry your physical self. Your physiology is what customers see and feel when they meet you for the first time. It's your physical enthusiasm and warmth they see and feel as you approach them; it's the confidence and assurance they see in your smile and feel in the pressure that you apply when you shake hands. It's the respect they see in your facial expression as you listen to the things that are important to them.

The old cliché 'actions speak louder than words' is absolutely true when you are communicating with new homebuyers. Your actions turn customers on or off. It's as simple as that.

To achieve rapport with your customers, begin today to notice how you present yourself. Remember that each of your actions and expressions communicates your sincerity or lack thereof. Your actions communicate your desire to participate in your customers experience or simply administrate your selling process. The choice is yours to make – keep this thought in mind as you choose – you are always communicating.

Tonality

Your tonality accounts for 38% of impact on rapport. Tonality is the rate, pitch, timbre, pace and inflection of your voice. When you are enthused and confident, you probably talk faster with a cadence that lets family, friends and customers know you're glad to be with them. When you're feeling depressed, you probably talk slower, your voice deepens and your voice inflections communicate that something is bothering you. In other words, your tonality communicates your state of mind!

Customers want to be assisted by salespeople who are excited about the task at hand and those who put the customer's needs ahead of their own situations. Remember that you only get one chance to make a first impression. What customers hear can either excite them or depress them. Once again the choice is yours – you are always communicating.

Words

Words account for 7% of impact on rapport. During my *Building Results* seminars I ask the following question: *"If physiology and tonality account for 93% of the impact on rapport, does that make words more or less important?"*

Participants often say, *"Less important"*. Nothing could be further from the truth. Words are extremely important because your choice of words differentiates you from all other salespeople. Words break through all the clutter that fills a customer's mind as he or she considers all available housing alternatives. Words ignite the spark that leads to alignment and agreement and eventually to rapport. But it's not just any words. Your words must be well chosen, clear, concise, precise and to the point. Once again the choice is yours – you are always communicating.

Communication and New Home Selling

By now you probably are beginning to make the mental connection between effective communication and new home selling. If not, consider this exchange I had with my daughter.

I was working in my home office, and my daughter asked if I had time to go new car shopping with her. Leslie, 23 at the time and living at home, is a college graduate, an elementary school teacher and quite self-assured in most situations, so her request for assistance surprised me. When I asked her why she needed my help, her answer startled me. She looked me in the eye and calmly said, *"I hate salespeople."* She explained that salespeople always try to manipulate her, talk her into something that might not be right for her situation and influence her to spend more than she could afford.

Her answered intrigued me because she was only 23 years of age and had already formed an opinion about salespeople that she likely would carry with her forever. I explained that I was finalizing a sales proposal for a builder I was meeting with the next day and suggested she wait till the weekend or ask her mother.

She and my wife did buy a car that day. What kind of car do you think she purchased? You may have guessed: a Saturn. When you consider what she said about salespeople, the Saturn is a logical choice. With Saturn what you see is what you get. There is no negotiating, salespeople do not apply pressure, and, according to their television commercials, they treat you like family.

I tell you this story because many of your customers feel pretty much like my daughter. She grew up communicating with salespeople because she is part of the consumer generation. She has formed opinions and biases based upon all her interactions with salespeople. When she purchases anything she brings her feelings with her. I want you to consider the opinions and biases customers bring with them when you walk out to meet them for the first time. Never forget that your customers are watching and listening to see if you can be trusted or are you someone to be avoided.

Rule of Liking

Several years ago The Wall Street Journal carried a story that claimed the reason customers did not purchase was not because they didn't like the product or the price was too high but rather because they didn't like the salesperson.

There is a rule about 'liking' that can serve you well if you practice it. In order for people to like you, you first must like them. Begin today to practice the 'rule of liking' by demonstrating through your physiology, tonality and words that you want to help customers get what is important to them. The choice is yours – you are always communicating.

Mind and Body are Parts of the Same System

Several years ago I was conducting a seminar in Houston. The table and seating arrangements were set up in a U-shaped configuration. I prefer this lay out for smaller groups because it allows me to interact closely with participants who have questions. I can see their facial expressions, hear their words clearly and interpret their understanding by listening to voice inflections.

I was discussing the concept of mind and body and its relationship to new home selling. I asked the salespeople to close their eyes and visualize a car as it approached their model home. I suggested that the car was a dark blue Mustang convertible. Inside were the driver and one passenger – man and woman. I stated that the couple was in their late 20s, and as they exit the car you can see they move with enthusiasm and eagerness. I instructed the students to keep their eyes closed and in one word describe what they see as they look at this couple.

I let them consider my request for several more seconds and then told them to open their eyes and remain relaxed. I then asked the group to describe what they saw in their mind's eye.

One student said, "*I see someone who is important.*" Another said, "*I see someone I want to have a working relationship with.*" A third said, "*I see money.*" I asked for an explanation. The student replied: "*The money I see represents my paycheck and the simple fact is that the only way to get my paycheck is to sell them a new home. In other words, quid pro quo, help people get what they want and they in turn help me get what I want.*"

What do you see when people approach your model home? What image do you project in your mind's eye?

I agree with the salesperson that saw money. I believe I move toward the things I think about. If I am thinking about a working relationship, then I'll move toward having a working relationship with my customer. If I am thinking about a customer's importance, my actions toward him will be consistent with the thought of importance. In other words, if I am thinking about money, all my actions will move me toward my goal of earning the money.

Please don't think that I consider having a working relationship or seeing customers as important is wrong. The opposite is true. I believe that customers are important, and I will take all the necessary actions to demonstrate to customers that I want to have a working relationship with them. But I see those two motivations as a means to an end. In other words if money is my ultimate motivation then I will demonstrate through my words and actions that customers are important and as result I will develop a working relationship which leads me to money.

The purpose of this exercise was to make the connection between the mind and the body. As I stated in the first communication principle – you are always communicating. Here's a critical fact – the first person you communicate with is yourself. You are what you think about. If you think negatively about your customers, your physical actions will be consistent with your thoughts.

An example of this can be found in this statement 'buyers are liars'. Have you ever heard anyone describe customers this way? I'm sure you have and sometimes maybe for good reasons. But stop now and think about that statement. Do you want to do business with people who lie? Of course not, you want to sell homes to people who are honest. But if you believe 'buyers are liars,' doesn't it follow that your actions will move you away from customers rather than towards them?

My NLP training taught me that for every experience I have in my brain, I have an address for that experience in my body. In other words, if I am thinking negatively then my physiology will be consistent with my thoughts. My mind and body are parts of the same system; one does not act without the other.

It is vital to understand the relationship between these first two principles. The impression you make with a customer sets up your working relationship. That relationship leads you to the sale, and the sale leads you to compensation. And that is what selling is all about – the money! So begin today to be aware of your thoughts, because your actions are going to be consistent with those thoughts – mind and body are part of the same system.

Ride the Horse in the Direction It Is Going

New home selling is changing and your customers are causing this change. They are more educated, have more information resources available and have more builders to choose from. To succeed in today's evolving marketplace you must differentiate yourself from other salespeople. This requires a paradigm shift in your thinking, a shift from controlling to following and then leading.

The third communication principle puts into perspective a strategy that causes you to think and act differently. First let me explain what I mean by ride the horse in the direction it is going.

An experienced horse rider knows that a horse will resist attempts to control it until it is comfortable with the rider. Any attempt to control a horse before it wants to be controlled could end in the rider getting thrown off. In a way the customers you meet demonstrate similar behavior. Initially they do not want to be controlled. They want freedom to explore your homes and community to reach a comfort level consistent with their buying motivations. Any attempt to control them before they're ready could raise their defenses and cause them to move away from you. Its good communication strategy to follow customers in the direction they want to go, hence – ride the horse in the direction it is going.

You demonstrate the third communication principle when you ask questions and listen carefully to the response. For example: If you ask a customer *"How may I help you today?"* and you hear this response, *"I want to see your model homes,"* what should you do? Should you proceed immediately to the model home or ignore the request and ask other qualifying questions?

The answer is obvious; you should go to the model home. However, I've observed many of you ignore your customers' answers and continue forward with your qualifying questions. This is just about the worst thing you could do. Your customer has given you an honest answer – *"I want to see the model home"*. What you do with this answer determines your willingness to work with your customer's agenda. When you ignore the answer, you are demonstrating that you are not listening, and your sales agenda is more important than your customer's agenda.

NLP training teaches that the meaning of communication is the response you get. This is a very important concept because it puts into perspective your role as the communicator. When you communicate with someone, it's not what you say but rather how the other person interprets what you say. For example consider the following exchange between a salesperson and customer:

Salesperson: *"Please share with me what is important about the new home we will build for you?"*

Customer: *"Well, let me think. I want a large back yard, preferably with trees, so I can have some privacy."*

How did the customer interpret what the salesperson said? Did the customer interpret the word home to include the back yard? The answer is yes. For this customer the backyard and home are one and the same.

Did the salesperson get what she wanted from this exchange? The answer is yes and no. She learned that the customer wanted a large back yard with trees but she didn't discover what would be important about the home. In the salesperson's mind the home and homesite are two separate things because each has its own features and benefits.

At this point in the communication the salesperson has a choice to make. She can take the answer she was given and begin discussing her homesites or she can ignore what she heard and ask another question about the home.

What should her decision be? I hope you said, *"Go with what she was given by the customer,"* because there will be plenty of opportunities to ask questions about the home after she satisfies the customer's needs regarding the homesite. When you go with what you're given, you demonstrate that you are listening. There is nothing you can do for a customer that is more important than listen.

The ride the horse in the direction it is going communication principle is discussed in other chapters of *Building Results* because it's so important. When you meet a customer for the first time, you have only one chance to differentiate yourself from your competitors. I'm convinced that this clear and connected communication can do just that. It clearly demonstrates your desire to put the customer's agenda before your own selling agenda.

The Person with the Most Knowledge Will Have the Most Influence

You probably have the heard the adage 'knowledge is power'. What you may not have heard is that with knowledge you gain influence. Influence is what you want when you're selling new homes. Consider the following illustration and the importance of influence in the new home selling process.

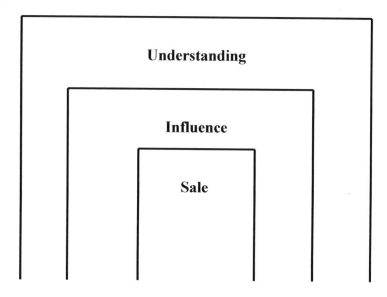

Rapport

Understanding

Influence

Sale

From this illustration you see that the sales process begins with rapport, moves to understanding, then to influence and finally to a sale.

The *Building Results'* sales process instructs you to find common ground that aligns you with your customer. Once you have identified with your customer, the next step is to ask questions to discover and understand what is important to your prospect. When you are able to demonstrate understanding, your customer will allow you to influence them toward a new home purchase.

It may sound simple, but it's not. It takes a great deal of preparation on your part to obtain the knowledge necessary to earn a customer's trust and confidence. I will more fully discuss the importance of this communication principal in Chapter 3. The important thing to know here is that knowledge is the key to influence. Remember – the person with the most knowledge will have the most influence.

The Map Is Not the Territory

Each of us has a view of reality that is our reality. Our reality is based on how we view the world. That view is a result of our own biases, our background, our learning and our experiences. Your customers also have a map that is based on their experiences. It is those experiences that your customers bring to the model home. Your responsibility is to discover the contents of your customer's map through precise questioning and then skillfully place them in the territory of your model homes, community and homesites. Once there you can add to your customers map by demonstrating all the values your builder has to offer.

However, you have learned through experience what a customer says isn't necessarily what a customer does. It is this action that confuses you and may cause you to lose a sale that you felt confident about. The following example may sound very familiar to you. I know that this happens frequently in every model home throughout America. The important thing to remember is that the fifth communication principle is working with you because it explains how your customers make a home buying decision.

I want you to visualize a family of four as they approach your model home; a mother, father and two young children. They approach the model home with enthusiasm.

The husband opens the door for his wife and children. You approach with a smile on your face and extend your hand to the husband and wife. You greet the children with a smile. You introduce yourself and the man introduces his family to you. You thank them for coming to the model home and ask how you may be of service today. The man answers that they would like to see your model home. You thank them for looking and ask a discovery question about their housing needs. The husband states that this is their first home and they need three or four bedrooms, two and one-half baths and a two-car garage. The wife adds they prefer the master bedroom on the first floor.

You verify the information and explain that the model home does not have a first-floor master but the children's rooms are separated from the master bedroom, affording the owners privacy and silence. They appear to be disappointed but agree to tour the model home.

You accompany the family, pointing out features and benefits and continuing to ask discovery questions. The children like the size of their bedrooms, the husband likes the large media room and the wife likes the kitchen/family-room layout. You ask several closing questions attempting to trial close them; however, the first floor master bedroom is a stumbling block.

The husband and wife agree to think it over and get back to you with a decision. You thank them for coming and ask if you may call tomorrow evening to answer questions and set up a second meeting. They agree and thank you for providing such good customer service.

The next evening you call and connect to their answering machine. You leave a message thanking them for visiting your community and request that they return your call at their earliest convenience. Another day passes and you decide to make a second follow up phone call. This time your prospects are home and are able to talk. You again thank them for visiting your community. You ask if they have any questions and attempt to set up a second visit.

The husband thanks you for the follow up call but proceeds to explain that they purchased a home last evening from a competitor. You are surprised and disappointed. You enquire about the home they purchased and you learn that the home has four bedrooms, all together on the second floor, no media room and the kitchen is separated from the family room. The home your prospect purchased is not what was described to you.

How is this possible? What happened? You know you listened carefully and thought you understood what was important to them. You know that you just lost a sale. What did you do wrong? The answer to that question is found in the fifth communication principle – the map is not the territory.

Your customers answered your discovery questions based on information that was available to them. When you ask a question the response you get is based on a person's experience. If the person is a second or third-time homebuyer the response you receive is rich with information. If the person has limited experience the response will reflect that. Therefore, a person's response to any question is predicated on what the individual has experienced.

You asked about housing needs and the husband and wife provided you with information they had agreed upon prior to the model home visit. This information represents the 'map' this family intends to follow in search of their first new home. Because it is their first home the information is limited because they have never experienced the new home buying process. Their answers to your questions provide you with direction similar to a map.

You took the customers' map and led them on a tour of the model home. Pointing out those things in the model that matched the map you were provided. In your mind you were following the directions you where given.

What you failed to understand is that the map you used can and frequently does change when the customer enters into the territory, i.e., the model home. Simply put – when a customer enters into your model home their experience changes. The customer sees things from a different perspective, a perspective that includes new experiences. Each new experience changes the customer's map. The more territory (builders and communities) the customer visits, the more the map changes.

This concept of 'map and territory' is critical to understand because your customer is constantly evolving and changing based upon the number of competitors they visit. According to national statistics the average new home prospect will visit six to ten communities before narrowing the selection down to two or three homes. Each new home and community visit is a new experience, which causes the map to change dramatically from the first to the tenth visit. How does this principle affect our presentation?

First, when you ask discovery and qualifying questions, be prepared to ask additional questions to uncover all the information included in your customer's map. In Chapter 5 you will learn how to ask precise discovery questions that will help you 'peel the onion' to uncover things that even your customer is not aware of. You want to understand and appreciate the map your customer is using as direction for finding their new home. The more you discover about your customers' needs, wants, and what is important, the more accurate you will be in demonstrating the right product, features, and options.

Second, once you ask your discovery questions and have listened carefully to your customer responses be ready to enter into the territory (model home and community) with your customer. Too many salespeople fail because they don't experience the model home with their customers.

Always remember that your customer is seeing the home and community for the first time. It is the first time your customer will experience the quality, features and options built into your homes. If you are not there you missed your chance to answer questions; you missed your customer's reaction to the product; and you missed the opportunity to discuss other available homes in case the model home does not meet wants and needs.

Once the customer enters into the model home new territory is being explored and experienced. Your customer's map is changing. To succeed in new home sales you must be part of your customer's total buying experience; you must be part of your customer's new ever-changing map. When selling new homes, keep in mind – the map is not the territory.

The Exception Is Not the Rule

The sixth and final communication principle 'the exception is not the rule' will help you deal positively with occasional adverse experiences.

You will meet many people during your career as a new home sales person, most of whom will treat you with respect. Occasionally some may treat you rudely. The sixth communication principle teaches you that those customers who treat you rudely are the exception and not the rule.

During my homebuilding career I have come to understand that some people are unhappy. These people are dissatisfied with their lives and want to transfer that unhappiness to others through words and actions. Fortunately, each of us has the option of whether to accept or reject their unhappiness. I know that those people were the exception and not the rule. I know that the majority of people I met wanted my help and treated me with kindness and respect.

I have learned to let go of what I can't control and to work with what I can. And so it should be with you. Your sales focus must be on those customers who come to you looking for solutions to their wants, needs and important issues. If you spend your valuable time attempting to change the exception you may miss those customers who need and want your help.

When the exception visits your model home, do everything possible to satisfy their needs and wants. But do not take their negative behavior personally. It is not you they are rejecting; rather it is their strategy to keep people at a distance. The exception wants to be left alone and nothing you do will change that behavior. Your best strategy is to remain calm, be available to answer questions and provide the necessary information so they can make an informed decision. This strategy allows you to focus on your job while providing a pleasant sales experience.

Fortunately, the exception is just an exception. Keep reminding yourself that most of the people you meet want and need your help. Focus on those customers, give them the best you can and you will realize new home sales success. Always keep in mind – the exception is not the rule.

Summary

Humans are complicated beings, so communication between us is complicated. It takes a lot of work to master these skills. Communicating with your significant other is a great example of the difficulty in listening carefully, reading physiology, interpreting accurately and responding thoughtfully. For those of us with children, especially teenagers, the challenge is exponential. Understanding those around you, including your customers, requires constant attention to your listening and interpreting skills.

As a sales professional your problem is even more complicated because you have to work hard to build positive habits and a superior mental framework inside your brain to project what will truly make you successful. You must master your knowledge, your physiology, your vocabulary, your habits, opinions and even your voice.

My goal is to provide you with the means to master those things by providing the ultimate new home selling 'How To' book. Beginning with Chapter 4 you will learn how to develop a seamless sales presentation that works with each and every customer you meet. You will be taught to do the right things at the right time; you will be taught to do the right things with precision; and you will be taught to do the right things consistently.

Your challenge is to read each chapter with an open mind and begin to integrate the ideas into your sales presentation. If you are a rookie to new home sales I suggest you read each chapter in order but if you are an experienced salesperson feel free to skip around. My only request is that you ask the precise questions included throughout this book exactly as they are written. These questions have been tested and they work. Remember that if you change the precise question, you most likely, will change the result. Get ready for a wonderful journey toward new home selling success.

Good luck and good selling!

Chapter 3

Preparation

Several years ago I was in my car listening to talk radio on my way to conduct a sales training seminar for a builder in Las Vegas. The announcer I was listening to was talking about 600 high school seniors that were not going to graduate because they had failed a 8th grade reading competency test nine times. He explained that this group of seniors had failed the reading test once in their 8th grade year and two times a year from their freshman through senior year. This story has stayed with me for many years because I know that those 600 students may be doomed to mediocrity because they lack the basic knowledge to read. And without that knowledge they limit their chance for personal success.

While this is a sad story it can serve as a catalyst for you to do everything possible to gather the knowledge you need to communicate effectively and efficiently with your new home prospects. Rest assured it will be your knowledge that causes your prospects to trust the words you speak and the actions you take. Knowledge gives you credibility. It is the pathway to influence, and influence leads to new home sales success.

Always remember this important fact: to your prospective buyer, you are the company. You're the person who must inspire confidence, trust, and credibility. You are the person who must reflect honesty, integrity, stability, dependability, caring and professionalism. You are the one who must relate personally to each prospect.

To achieve these extraordinarily challenging goals, you must really know yourself. You must build on your natural strengths while developing knowledge and skills to become the complete professional. To do so you face another exceptional challenge: being honest with yourself about your strengths and weaknesses. Then you must take positive steps that strengthen your knowledge, skills and overall performance.

The following information outlines the basic knowledge you need to communicate and build credibility with your customers. Gathering this information is not easy. It will take you time and effort but the knowledge you gather will differentiate you from your competition. You will meet your prospects with confidence and enthusiasm and that will mean additional sales and income for you. Be patient with this assignment – don't get discouraged if the information is hard to find – chunk the assignment into small pieces and before you know it you have acquired all the knowledge you need to influence people to buy from you. New home sales success starts today, don't delay!

Product Knowledge – Builder

When someone is going to make what may be the single largest investment in his or her lifetime, trust is an issue, and builder knowledge is critical. Very few buyers really know enough about the various homebuilders they're considering to assess their reliability, integrity and commitment to customer satisfaction. It's a fundamental part of your job as salesperson to make your builder stand out positively and professionally from the competition. To do so you must have the following minimum information about the builder and be able to associate each with a specific benefit or benefits to the prospective buyer.

Critical areas of knowledge include length of time in business, financial strength, number of homes built annually, warranty and service policy and procedures, local or national management, and awards builder has received for outstanding customer service or unique style and design.

Product Knowledge – Builder Policies and Procedures

Over the years I have observed that in the area of builder policies and procedures, most building companies only pay lip service to this vitally important area. Unfortunately, most builders assume the salesperson will, on their own, take the time to learn the various procedures the builder uses to run the business. This is a tragic mistake that can lead to serious problems for the builder and salesperson. While I believe it is the builder's responsibility to provide the salesperson with a full orientation on policies and procedures I know that in most homebuilding companies it is up to the salesperson to gather that knowledge.

Whether you are an experienced veteran or a rookie take the time to meet with each department head and ask for the specific policies that are used to organize the running of that department. These meetings will provide you with the knowledge that will allow you to answer your customer's questions with confidence and enthusiasm. Keep in mind that the following is a partial list – each builder is different but it does provide a good place to start.

Critical areas of knowledge: sales agreements, earnest money, lot holds, conduct of employees, drugs and alcohol, performance appraisals, standards of business conduct, contract addenda, deposits, construction starts, customer relations, fair housing and contingencies.

Product Knowledge – Community

Every community is different. Each has its own strengths and weaknesses. It is up to you to gather the knowledge that defines those strengths and weaknesses. Take time to study your community always looking for those things that separate your community from the competition. Meet with the person who purchased the community and find out why the land was purchased. Talk to the customer's who have purchased and understand how and why they made the decision to purchase. People buy on emotion but they justify with facts. Find out what those facts are and then share them with your new customers. This builds trust and confidence in you and let's your customers know that others made the same decision they are making and for good reasons.

Critical community information includes unique selling propositions per homesite, probable streetscapes, use of adjacent parcels, closest service businesses, community covenants and restrictions, homesite availability, local amenities, owner or developer, site premiums and options per site.

Product Knowledge – Area

To be as effective as possible, and to achieve maximum respect and credibility with prospects, you must have the following information, at a minimum, committed to memory. Be prepared to set aside several days to complete this part of your knowledge gathering. And, where required, ask for written documentation to serve as third party testimonial. Place all this information into an Area Binder and set it out where prospects can see and read. Many home purchases are made because of the location and it is up to you to provide your customer with area information so they can make an informed decision.

My wife and I have made two home purchases because my wife wanted to be within the boundaries of a specific church. When I compared the homes, each had all the features we were looking for, but the one difference was the church. Be careful not to overlook the value of knowing your area and all its many benefits. It can mean the difference between making and losing a sale.

Essential school and community information includes location, national test scores, PTA president, principals, class size, phone numbers, facilities, shopping, fire and police departments, major traffic accesses, public transportation, recreation areas, tax information, service businesses, travel times to key locations and utility services.

Product Knowledge – Homes and Options

Product knowledge of homes and options is a must. If you fail to understand your product, you will fail.

When you meet prospects for the first time understand that they are there to compare homes. They are not there to answer questions about their personal lives. They are there to compare what you're offering versus the competition. Then they will compare both your product and the competition's to what they currently own or have in mind. If you can point out the benefits of your homes, your chances of closing the sale increase greatly.

Take time to meet with the builder's architect and acquire as much product knowledge as you can. Ask about buyer profiles, room layouts, and design options. Meet with the purchasing and estimating department manager and ask questions about the various products included in the homes. Learn about each product's features and benefits. If necessary, request the phone number of the product supplier and call to secure information on what makes their product unique and different.

Keep this thought in mind, model homes represent three things: product, features and options. If you are not able to communicate the value of those three things you will fail. Gather information about your product, features and options and you will succeed.

Critical information includes square footage of each house, square footage of the living space, square footage of each room, options available per home and per home and homesite combination, product features and benefits, prices, unique selling propositions per floor plan and itemized cost of home ownership per plan.

Product Knowledge – Homesites

Tom Richey, a legend in new home sales training, is credited with saying, "*Get your customers to the homesite and you will write*". I believe, based on my experience, no truer words have been spoken. Unfortunately, his words for the most part fall on deaf ears. Most new home salespeople fail to take people to homesites. I believe this occurs because salespeople do not take the time to study and gather knowledge about their homesites. No one wants to place themselves in a position to demonstrate what they don't know so they eliminate this important part of the sales presentation and that is a shame.

The late Dave Stone, another legend in new home sales training believed that every homesite was one-of-a-kind. He taught that every homesite had its own uniqueness, and it was up to the salesperson to discover that uniqueness and share it with prospects.

Meet with your community builder or sales manager and walk each homesite asking questions about the value of one homesite over the other. Armed with this information include the homesite visit into every new home sales presentation. I promise that this will differentiate you from your competition.

Important homesite information includes the size of each homesite, acceptable homes and options per site, location of the building envelope, compass directions for sun orientation, driveway location, community map, unique selling propositions per homesite, premiums, precise corners, tree inventory, and possible walkout availability from basements.

Product Knowledge – Financing

Most homebuyers must acquire a loan to purchase a new home. This fact provides you with a unique opportunity to demonstrate knowledge in an area that can be very complicating. Meet with loan officers and ask them to explain the various finance programs and find out the positive and negatives of each program.

Let your prospects know during your sales presentation that you know of several financing programs that will meet their specific needs. When you demonstrate knowledge in this vital area you continue to build the trust and confidence a prospect needs to purchase a home.

When you fail to understand the critical elements of new home financing you are leaving your chance for success up to chance. Make the right choice – learn all you can about new home financing including these subjects: available program types and rates, qualifying criteria, appropriate ratios, approval times and credit repair.

Product Knowledge – Handling Resistance

No community is perfect. Each has features that may seem less than desirable, some to a significant percentage of your prospects. You must identify these issues and carefully prepare a strategy for handling this resistance before you are face-to-face with a customer. In Chapter 9 you're given a process for handling customer resistance. The chapter includes forms that should be completed before you meet your customers. By completing this exercise you prepare yourself to meet a customer's resistance head-on. In fact, you welcome the resistance because you know resistance is a stepping stone to the close.

Take a critical look at each of the following six areas: homes, homesites, community, location, financing, and builder. Look for things that your customers may find objectionable. Ask your spouse, family, friends, and Realtors to critically review these areas and to provide honest feedback. The best way to handle customer resistance is to be prepared for it. Gathering this knowledge helps you prepare a strategy that will provide your customers with facts that overcome any points of resistance.

Possible areas of resistance include: homes, home sites, community, location, financing and builder.

Knowledge of Competition

If ever there was a true adage in new home sales, it is 'knowledge is power'. You cannot optimize sales unless you know your competitors as well as you know your own builder.

The minimum data that you should keep current includes the following: community, products and floor plans, prices and price per square foot, standard features and options, quality of home sites, delivery times, incentives to purchase, financing and sales staff.

It has been said, and it is true that the only thing you cannot match is people. A competing builder can match your price, your product, and your promotions, but he can't match you. Take time to study the salesperson you are competing against, know his or her selling strengths and weaknesses. Capitalizing on a person's weakness may be the difference between success and failure in your community.

Examining Yourself and Your Surroundings

Now that we've examined the knowledge necessary for you to position yourself for success, I want you to consider the personal things you must do to be successful. The following identifies not only the things you must do but also the things your customer sees when they meet you for the first time, things that tell the customer a great deal about you and your community. Ask yourself: *"Am I setting myself up for success or for failure?"* Take a look at yourself and your surroundings; would you want to do business with you?

Preparing Yourself

Prepare a specific plan for each day with a specific time noted for each activity. Have specific priorities for each day, starting with the most important and/or difficult items. Remember Paretto's 80/20 Rule. 80% of your results are generated by 20% of your activities. Do the critical 20% first! Average performers wallow in the 80% non-critical items and are forever doomed to mediocrity.

Remember that you will live-up to your own expectations. So start building your day's positive attitude by setting your expectations high. Always aim to play over your head. It's the only way to win in new home selling.

Does your dress and general appearance help project the image of a successful, competent, trustworthy professional? Remember first impressions are extremely important. So be honest. What could you change that would predispose prospective buyers to like, trust and respect you more? What can you change to your advantage?

Is your car neat and clean? Does it reflect a sales professional? If not, make it a habit of regularly detailing your car both inside and outside. Does your car have four doors? If not, consider purchasing one because it provides the room and comfort most customers expect and deserve.

Sales Center Preparation

First impressions are lasting impressions. Begin each work day by asking yourself the following questions. Is my sales center clean? Is everything orderly and neat? Are all sales and closing forms readily available? Have you positioned registration forms and brochures where they can be used most effectively? Remember that the environment you create reflects you. You hardly create a sense of confidence and trust if the sales center is not properly refreshed or you're fumbling through stacks of paper or drawers to find things.

Are all doors, windows, lights, etc., in proper working order? If not, get things fixed immediately. If you've been working from the same sales center for some time, have you done anything to refresh it to help maintain your own enthusiasm and frame of mind while you're there?

The sales center and model is your store. Much of your success is dependent on how you take care of your store. People want to do business with professionals – your sales center tells your prospect what they can expect from you. Remember first impressions are lasting impressions. Make your first impression a 'wow impression'.

Physical Environment of Sales Center

People want to do business with successful people. If you have evidence of success in selling homes, such as awards, diplomas, and third-party testimonials, position them where your customers can see them.

If your builder has won awards from the local builders' association of the National Association of Home Builders, display them proudly. Awards provide a perception that your builder is a company of integrity and stability. Don't put them in a desk drawer. Position them where everyone can see them and maybe inquire about them.

If your community is selling fast, create a sense of urgency to act now. Many salespeople I know leave completed contracts on their desktops to demonstrate that homes are selling fast.

When you receive third party testimonial letters from satisfied customers, place them in a three-ring binder. Position the binder where all your customers can read what satisfied customer are saying about you and your builder. Be proud of your accomplishments; never forget people want to do business with successful people and companies.

Maintaining the Model Home

Everything in the model must work properly, without squeaks, scrapes or undue force. This includes lights, floors, windows, stairs, doors, cabinets and faucets. If not, get the item replaced or fixed immediately. Models must be exceptionally clean, both inside and out. They must be maintained continuously.

Remember that marketing studies continuously confirm that most buyers expect their home will have less quality than the models.

Essential sales forms and other materials should be carefully placed wherever they may be required. You never know when a prospect will be ready to say yes. Keep contracts in your car and carry them with you when you visit inventory homes. This simple act demonstrates professionalism and expectation. In Chapter 10 you will learn that assumption is the most powerful close of all. By having contracts with you, you are assuming the sale.

All signage must be properly placed. Signs must be replaced when worn, damage, defaced or no longer applicable. One thing all prospects do before meeting you for the first time is tour the community. If your signs are lying dirty and faded in the weeds, you are sending a negative message to your prospects, a message that can cost you business.

Landscaping around the models and inventory homes should be maintained regularly. This is a benefit not only to new customers but also the buyers who have already purchased. As builders we have a responsibility to maintain the community and insure increasing property values. Always remember to be a good neighbor.

The Community

As a good neighbor you must work with the production department to keep streets, entrance areas and homesites clean and well-maintained. Ask your builder to keep weeds on lots trimmed and streets free from mud and construction debris. Communicate with production personnel to insure that trailers, compounds and garbage facilities are properly maintained and reasonably clean.

Some builders I know make it a practice to clean all inventory homes and streets on Friday before weekend traffic. This is a good practice because research suggests that home buyers relate cleanliness with quality. The cleaner the community, the easier it is to sell new homes.

Knowledge – The Foundation of New Home Sales Success

Earlier in this chapter I discussed the adage that 'knowledge is power'. There's another saying that is equally applicable: 'knowledge is potential power'. The knowledge you gather will be powerful only if you use it. If you gather all the knowledge outlined in this chapter and don't use it, then all you've done is waste your time.

The knowledge gathered in this chapter represents the foundation on which all other chapters in *Building Results* are built. Your sales presentation, the answers you provide, the values you build around your products and options, and your responses to customer objections, all are linked to your knowledge of your homes, homesites, community, location, financing and builder.

When you take time to understand the value of those things you earn the right to ask for the order. Fail to gather knowledge, and you limit your chance for success. Gather the knowledge outlined in this chapter and you have positioned yourself for success.

Good luck and good selling!

Chapter 4

Connecting

In the critical path selling process one of the first things you learn is greeting. What I want you to consider is that greeting is part of a bigger process called *Connecting*.

This chapter examines the entire process of *Connecting*. The ideas contained in this chapter will cause you to reconsider everything you have been taught about greeting. Read with an open mind taking time to reflect on all the possibilities that are know open to you because you expanded the greeting to include all six elements that make up the *Connecting* process.

These six elements will demonstrate the value of the first, second, and third communication principles; so get ready for a journey that is sure to make new home selling fun, easy, and more financially rewarding.

The six distinct elements that make up the *Connecting* process are attitude, sales presentation, rapport, determining needs, understanding the importance of time and the greeting. The following examines each element to determine how it can enhance your effectiveness.

Attitude

A positive mental attitude is essential to success in new home selling. To be effective, your attitude must demonstrate these qualities:

1. A strong sense of pride in your builder, the product and the people with whom you work.

2. A sense of understanding and appreciation for the customer.

3. A sense of confidence in your own selling skills.

This combination of positive factors brings consistent effectiveness. A positive attitude begins with self-motivation. You cannot sell new homes with a negative attitude. Homebuyers have their own fears and uncertainties – they do not need yours. One solution is to keep your immediate sales objectives in mind. The builder is properly concerned about long-range objectives, but you must be concerned about making and closing sales now. Concentrate on today. Learn to love the customer you are with today!

To make my point I want to share with you an experience I had with a large national home builder that specializes in senior housing. I was retained to work independently with each salesperson. My assignment was to shadow the salesperson, observe a sales presentation, and then meet with the salesperson and coach them on how they might improve the effectiveness of their presentation.

Each salesperson met their client and demonstrated skill in greeting and asking several excellent qualifying questions. They then released the customer to walk through and experience the model homes unattended. This behavior was consistent with each salesperson. When I asked the salespeople why they let the customer go through the model homes unescorted, they replied, "*If I go through the models, I might miss my next up.*"

These salespeople were letting go of a possible sale to wait on something that may or may not be as good or even appear! They were losing sight of their sales objective because they were more concerned with what they might miss.

Is it possible you are demonstrating similar behavior? I ask you because a big part of a positive attitude is expecting to sell – not just some of the time but all of the time. When you release a customer you are letting go of your opportunity. You are leaving your success to the chance that the customer will return to you. Begin today to make it a practice to stay with your prospect until you have completed a full sales presentation. Do this consistently, sales will improve, and you will have a consistent positive attitude.

Don't Be Afraid to Fail

Too many sales representatives give in at the first sign of adversity. Be aware that the homebuyer has a buying process just like you have a selling process. And part of the buying process is to eliminate you. Remember you stand in the way of the homebuyer looking at the model home. Some customers will throw up all sorts of roadblocks to deflect your sales presentation.

If you recognize this as part of buying and not indifference to you personally, your attitude will reflect acceptance and a willingness to help. Persistence brings results, so don't give up or retreat from a difficult sales situation. Don't allow fear of failure to control your attitude.

Maintain a Positive Self-Image

You achieve what you expect to achieve. A positive attitude evident in the mental picture you have of yourself is transmitted to others through your actions – mind and body are part of the same system.

Set up an inventory of your talents and abilities. List those positive attributes you know you have and then make a decision to strengthen them. True, you should spend some time each day focusing on your weaknesses, but you must direct most of your energy to building on your strengths.

Remember Pareto's rule that 80% of your results are generated by 20% of your activities. Pareto's 80/20 rule also applies to strengths and weaknesses. So start today and analyze your talents and abilities; then focus on what you do best. The result will be improved performance, customer satisfaction and additional sales and income.

Appreciate and Understand Your Customer

It's important to communicate concern for your customers' needs. They want to do business with someone who respects them and genuinely cares about what is important to them.

In an issue of a popular homebuilder magazine, new homebuyers were asked, *"What do you want from your salesperson?"* Responses were simple and straightforward: *"I want honest and accurate information about the homes and community. I want the salesperson to respect my needs, wants and what is important to me."*

Remember that home buying is a monumental decision for most people. It represents a major change in lifestyle and is probably the largest single purchase someone will ever make. That's why it's essential for you to understand needs and to appreciate fears and concerns.

Build Confidence in Your Selling Skills

Customers want you to care about their needs, but they also want you to be competent enough to help them. Customers prefer to do business with competent professionals. The following items were discussed in Chapter 2, but because they're so important, I feel they are worth repeating.

First, improve both your community and location knowledge. You're not just selling a house; you're offering a way of life. Learn about schools, shopping, transportation, medical facilities, recreational opportunities and local taxes – every facet of community living.

Second, know your product. Not only do you need to know your builders' features and selling points but you need a good basic understanding of home construction so you'll be able to explain the pros and cons of each building technique. Spend time with your community's building supervisor and visit houses in various stages of construction so you'll know how your homes are built.

Third, know your homesites. Each homesite in your community is unique, a one-of-a-kind. Walk each homesite and list the advantages to buying a particular lot. Be prepared to discuss each site at a moment's notice. Homebuyers respond favorably when they perceive you know what you are talking about.

Fourth, understand your builders' policies and procedures. Don't promise something your builder can't deliver. Most people will understand the need for rules and policies, so be honest and upfront about them. Customers do not want to be misled, nor do they want you to misrepresent what the builder can or cannot do. Don't forget that you are the expert in the eyes of the customer; you represent the builder, and it's essential that you know and appreciate your builder's policies and procedures.

Fifth, increase your knowledge of financing. It isn't necessary to have an advanced degree in economics, but you should know the mortgage market well and have a fundamental grasp of financing alternatives to ensure that the information you give your customers is current and accurate.

Sixth, know your competition. Know what's available, what it costs and how it compares with your builder's product. Visit competing model homes and evaluate the differences between each community. Compare location, land plan, your builder's history and reputation, housing design, construction and financial backing. Understand, too, that competition comes from many quarters, not just other new homes, and you need to know the advantages and disadvantages of housing alternatives such as the following: purchasing a used home, staying put, waiting to tour other homes, renting and remodeling.

Sales Presentation

Many sales representatives think of the sales presentation as little more than their sales pitch. But the presentation is much more comprehensive. It encompasses the way the builder, the community, the models and you are presented to potential customers. It is the image or impression that you and your builder project to the public.

Naturally, you want to be sure that your first impression is positive. If not, what your customers see and experience will leave them with no desire to return. That's why your total sales environment must generate a positive force.

Begin With the Community

Look at the entire community through the eyes of your customers and ask yourself if you would buy a house in this community?

Since first impressions set the mood for the sales presentation, make sure that directions to the subdivision and models are accurate and well-maintained. See that all model signs are painted and installed properly. Be sure that the landscaping is immaculate, that the grass around the entrance and models is mowed regularly, that homesites are free of weeds, underbrush and other obstructions and have proper signage.

Maintain the Models

Model homes are vitally important to your efforts. Not only do they serve as a showcase for your builder's product, features, and options but they offer the customer a tangible representation of what their new home will be like.

In short, they compensate for the customer's lack of imagination – models sell the 'feeling'. That's why model homes must look their best at all times. Are they clean and neat, inside and out? Are they well-maintained? Do all features and systems operate flawlessly? Are displays and selling aids complete and up-to-date?

Take a Look at Yourself

It's not enough to offer a fine community and excellent homes. You, too, must reflect an image of professionalism. The manner in which you dress, talk, and act is just as important as the housing values you represent.

The extra time you devote to being well-groomed will not only improve your image in the eyes of others but will also help you to feel more confident. The message is clear: If you want people to listen to you and place confidence in you, dress and carry yourself in a manner that speaks of authority.

Building Rapport

By becoming more aware of both your own communication patterns and those of the people you must deal with, you greatly increase your personal selling success.

My NLP training taught me that when people identify with each other, they cooperate. The best way to identify with another person is through rapport. Rapport signals a relationship exemplified by agreement, alignment, or likeness and similarity. To the extent that you are in agreement or alignment – verbally and nonverbally – with another person or bear some likeness to that person, you are in a state of rapport with that person.

In order to meet new customers on their own level you must be flexible. In all forms of communication, the individual with the widest range of responses controls the communication. If you have more variety in your behavior than the other person, then you can control your interaction with that person. Having enough range in your own behavior to match and even exceed the other person's range is the foundation on which rapport is built, and building rapport is the best tool for overcoming a customer's resistance to what you want them to do.

The following NLP rapport building techniques will enhance your range of flexibility and enable you to meet new customers on their own level.

Pacing

Pacing is a skill that involves meeting your customer where he or she is right now, reflecting back what you know to be true, or matching some part of your customer's ongoing experience. It involves presenting to another person those aspects of you that are most nearly like those of that person. When you pace a customer, you are in effect saying, *"I'm like you. You're safe with me. You can trust me."* Pacing helps establish trust and credibility.

You can pace a customer's body language and speech pattern, including rate of speech, tonality and volume, and the words and phrases a customer uses.

When you're in step with your customer, you can guide her with your next step. It seems paradoxical at first, but one of the best ways to change a customer's behavior is to first synchronize with some aspect of her behavior (pace it), and then gradually evolve or change your actions so that the customer follows your lead.

Leading

When you have achieved rapport with a customer, the customer is apt to follow the next step you take. To get a customer to follow you, utilize the following strategy:

Pacing  Leading

Pacing is doing something similar to what the customer is doing; leading is doing something different from what the customer is doing. The best strategy is to pace first and then lead. Meet your customer where he or she is and then suggest other options. The general rule is that if the customer resists your lead, go back to pacing and look for new opportunities to lead after agreement and/or alignment has been reestablished.

Most selling situations involve a continual process of pacing and leading until a satisfactory outcome is achieved. The following graphic illustrates that point.

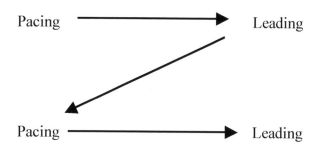

Body Matching

Body matching and gesture matching are the most powerful elements to match for building rapport quickly. In Chapter 2 you might remember the following chart illustrating the three different communication elements you can pace and how each impacts rapport. Study this chart and understand the significance your physiology, tonality and words have on your ability to establish and maintain rapport.

Communication Element	% of Impact on Rapport
Physiology	55%
Tonality	38%
Words	7%

As you can see from the chart, physiology, or body matching, has the most impact. You can match your customer whether they are sitting, standing or walking through a model with you. When you are standing with a customer and they are concentrating on a floor plan or a homesite map, you can stand as they stand. Your customers' peripheral vision and their unconscious will pick up the sameness, and they will feel comfortable with what you are doing.

You can match gestures. When customers want to place emphasis on a point they are making, they use their hands to do it. For example, if they want to communicate a certain size lot, they will spread their hands apart to show you size. To demonstrate understanding, all you have to do is indicate the size of the lot by spreading your hands apart. They will look at your hands and nod in agreement. This simple act of gesture matching demonstrates sameness, similarity and understanding.

Body matching is an unconscious process. If you are having a really good conversation with someone, just stop for a second and notice. You are probably already standing or gesturing in a similar way.

Verbal Matching

Another powerful communication element to match is your prospect's tonal or verbal language. You can match rate of speech, pitch, inflections, timbre or volume.

Never match a person's geographical accent or speech impediment, but you can find some part of that accent, such as rate or inflection, that you can match. Accents and even impediments have a certain rhythm to them that you can match and yet remain subtle.

Auditory matching can be used with the hurry-up customer or with someone who is angry or aggressive. Here are some examples that help make the point.

A hurry-up customer's tonal qualities are at a faster rate, erratic rhythm and maybe even a higher pitch and timbre. You can greet a hurry-up prospect by matching pace and rhythm, and then, using pacing and leading, you can begin to slow down your pace and rhythm, a little at a time. You can add body matching to enhance the process. When you have significantly paced your customer, you may begin to slow down; your customer will match you and slow down.

Angry customer's tonal qualities are faster rate, fast rhythm, loud volume, and possibly high pitch. You can pace back the rate, rhythm, volume and timbre but never the emotion. As you pace the tonal qualities, you can say positive and directive words, leading your customer toward a resolution to the problem. Find out what's wrong and tell your customer what you can do to solve the problem. Never lie or provide misleading information. Remember that rapport creates trust and credibility.

Preferred Communication Mode

In order to get a customer to understand what you mean, you first need to learn how your customer understands, or at least how your customer tries to understand.

People represent language in the five senses. The brain takes in information through the five senses. We see, hear, feel, smell and taste the world around us. After processing the information in our brains, we re-represent the information to others through language.

Each person you meet has a dominant or preferred mode of communication. When you make initial contact with new customers, they will probably be thinking in one of three main representational systems: generating visual images, having feelings, talking or listening. You can discover which representational system your customer is using by listening to the words they choose. Here are some examples:

Visual bias: *"I see what you mean"*

Auditory bias: *"Tell me again what you mean"*

Feeling bias: *"That idea just feels right to me"*

Identifying which communication mode is dominant for your customers at any given time is an important key to their pattern of understanding and is therefore an important element both in understanding them and getting them to understand you. The message is clear, when you use a customer's dominant communication mode, they will respond. It is not important that you are able to tell which mode the customer prefers but that you have the ability to recognize which mode they are using at that moment and match back with the words you use.

Sensory System Words

Predicates are the process words (verbs, adverbs and adjectives) that people use to represent their experience internally, either visual, auditory, kinesthetic, gustatory or olfactory. Below are listed some of the more commonly used words in each sensory system.

Visual (see)

analyze	examine	image	picture	survey
angle	focus	inspect	pinpoint	vague
appear	foresee	look	scene	view
aspect	glance	notice	scope	vision
clarity	hindsight	obscure	scrutinize	watch
cognizant	horizon	observe	see	witness

Auditory (say or hear)

announce	earshot	mention	rumor	state
articulate	enunciate	noise	say	talk

audible	gossip	oral	screech	tell
boisterous	hear	proclaim	shrill	tone
hush	pronounce	silence	utter	converse
inquire	remark	sound	vocal	discuss

Kinesthetic (feel or do)

active	flow	hustle	set	affected
foundation	intuition	shallow	bearable	grasp
lukewarm	shift	callous	grip	motion
softly	charge	hanging	muddled	solid
concrete	hassle	panicky	sore	emotional
heated	pressure	stir	feel	hold

Olfactory (smell)

aroma	essence	raunchy	smells	bouquet
fragrance	pungent	stench	dank	musty
reeks	stinks	dusty	odor	rotten

Gustatory (taste)

bitter	flat	sour	tangy	bland
salty	spicy	tasty	burnt	sharp
sweet	zesty	delicious		

Sensory System Phrases
Visual (see)

an eyeful	appears to me	shadow of a doubt
bird's eye view	catch a glimpse of	clear-cut
dim view	eye to eye	flashed on
get a perspective	get a scope on	hazy idea
well-defined	in light of	in person
in view of	looks like	make a scene

Auditory (hear)

afterthought	blabbermouth	clear as a bell
clearly expressed	call on	describe in detail
earful	express yourself	give account of
give me your ear	grant an audience	heard voices

| hold your tongue | idle talk | inquire into |
| keynote speaker | loud and clear | speaking out |

Kinesthetic (feel)

all washed up	boils down to	chip off the old block
come to grips with	control yourself	cool/calm/collected
firm foundation	floating in air	get a handle on
get a load of this	get in touch with	get the drift of
get your goat	hand-in-hand	hang in there
heated argument	hold it	hold on

The object of matching words is to pace or match the language in which your customer speaks, thus creating an atmosphere of trust and credibility. The following is a verbal matching example. The purpose is to demonstrate how you can match your customer's language patterns. The key to success in verbal matching is listening for the visual, auditory or kinesthetic words your customers use. In this example I have underlined the words that can be matched to establish rapport thereby aligning you with your customer.

Salesperson: *Hi, welcome to XYZ Homes. How may I be of service to you today?*

Visual Customer: *We just want to <u>look</u> today.*

Salesperson: *Great, thanks for <u>looking</u> here, what would you like to <u>see</u> first?*

Auditory Customer: *We <u>heard</u> some good things about your homes and we wanted to <u>talk</u> to you about some of the models.*

Salesperson: *Well, thank you, it's great to <u>hear</u> that people are <u>saying</u> good things about XYZ Homes. I'll <u>tell</u> you a little about each model, and then you can <u>tell</u> me which ones that you would like to <u>discuss</u> further?*

Kinesthetic Customer: *We were <u>driving</u> in the area and we just want*
to get a <u>feel</u> for the homes you <u>build</u>.

Salesperson: *Great, thanks for <u>coming</u> to XYZ Homes. We can <u>walk</u>*
through the models and really provide you with a good <u>feel</u>
for what we are offering.

Now it is your turn. Take five minutes to complete the following verbal matching exercise. Read the sentence in italics several times. Underline the visual, auditory, kinesthetic, gustatory or olfactory word used in the sentence.

Your assignment is to select from the four sentences the one that uses visual, auditory, kinesthetic, gustatory or olfactory words that matches the first sentence. Keep in mind that more than one sentence may match the first sentence.

Matching Exercise
A. That other builder just did not listen to what I was saying!
1. I don't grasp what you mean.
2. That is not how we treat our customers.
3. Sounds to me as if we need to discuss what you want.
4. It appears to me that we need to talk this out.
B. This model just doesn't seem to click.
1. I noticed that.
2. What specifically doesn't ring a bell?
3. What do you mean?
4. Let's get a grip on what doesn't seem to fit.
C. Salespeople just give me a lot of static.
1. Some of them are just a lot of noise, but at XYZ Homes we listen to our customers.
2. Some can make you feel uncomfortable, but at XYZ Homes we do what is necessary to please our customers.
3. So, you think sales people are unreasonable.
4. Oh, I hear what you are saying.
D. I can't seem to focus on how I feel about this home.
1. It sounds to me that we need to get a handle on the situation.
2. What else do you need to see in here to feel comfortable with it?

3. What is it about this home that is not in tune with what you want?
4. What do you need to add to this home to feel comfortable?
E. This house is so warm and comfortable!
   1. Yes, it has a beautiful and rich design.
   2. It is one of our best designs.
   3. A lot of people say that when they come in here.
   4. Yes, it was built with that in mind.
F. I'm looking for a home with a beautiful view and lots of windows.
   1. Lots of windows and a view give the home a spacious feeling.
   2. I can show you some sites on this map that have beautiful views and the floor diagram here illustrates that our models have lots of windows.
   3. I know I can find a lot on the site map that will have a beautiful view and lots of windows.
   4. Oh yes, lots of windows sounds lovely, and I can tell you which site will give you the nicest view.

(Answers – A – 3, B – 2 or 4, C – 1 or 2, D – 2, E – 1 or 4, F – 2)

How did you do? Where you able to pick out the sensory based words? The challenge in verbal matching is to train yourself to listen for how your customer prefers to communicate. Does your customer have a visual, auditory, kinesthetic, gustatory, or olfactory preference?

One thing that may simplify this skill is that when new customers visit the model for the first time; most likely, they will be using either, visual or kinesthetic words. The reason is that most customers initially only want to look and get a feel for the home. Once they like what they see and it compares with what they have in mind they will want to talk with you. Therefore, train yourself to listen for visual and kinesthetic words initially. Once you have that skill down add listening for auditory, gustatory, and olfactory words. It may sound difficult but once you train yourself to listen for sensory based words you will be amazed at how easy it is to establish and maintain rapport.

Minimal Clues

Have you ever thought a sales presentation was going really well and then the customer thanked you for the information and walked out? Did you ever go through some information that may have had several points and as you got to the last point, your customer asked you, "*What was that first point you made?*" Did you ever talk for hours with a customer to find out that they were sold after the first half-hour and you could have closed the sale sooner?

In each of these situations you were probably concentrating very hard on the content of your sales presentation rather than focusing on your customer. When the focus is taken off the customer, you can lose sight of valuable information. Remember that customers have their own agendas, and when you are focused on your agenda, you may miss vital cues that assist you in deciding what selling strategy to employ.

These cues are called minimal cues. They are small movements that your customer makes that let you know that something in their experience has changed. Minimal cues happen whether something good or bad has happened. The cue denotes a change in thinking or attitude. It is up to you to first notice the change, then stop where you are and ask a question that will tell you the information you need to know about the change. Consider asking any of the following questions when you notice a difference:

"Is everything OK?"

"Do you have a question you would like to ask?"

"Am I going too fast? Would you like for me to slow down?"

"Are we running out of time? I noticed you looked at your watch. Do you have to leave?"

Here are examples of minimal cues:

Stepping back away from you	Leaning back away from you
Head tilt	Head jerk
Facial color change	Raised eyebrow
Lip pout	Voice tone shift
Voice rate shift	Voice volume shift

The following exchange between the salesperson and customer demonstrates how to respond to minimal cues:

Salesperson: *"Here are the two floor plans that are available with this model."*

Customer:	*(Scrunches up forehead) "Oh, they are very nice. Well, I think I'll look around a little more."*
Salesperson:	*(Notices customer's forehead — paces back the forehead scrunch subtlety). "Is there something else you would rather see in the design of your new home?"*
Customer:	*"Well, these two floor plans don't show a game room and I need a big room for the children to play in. I just assumed that all new homes had game rooms."*
Salesperson:	*"When you look up here, you can see that there is one more bedroom here than you need. I can request a change to finish the room so it will be right next to their bedroom."*
Customer:	*"Well that is a possibility. Let me call my husband and see if he can come over now."*

The more you practice noticing minimal cues, the more you'll realize the power behind this matching strategy. You can use minimal cues to determine how the presentation is going and receive information you may have been missing.

Change the Way You See – Change the Way You Sell

There are two ways to look at your customers. You can choose to emphasize the differences between you and your customer. Or you can choose to emphasize the similarities – the things you share. If you emphasize the differences, you will find it hard to establish rapport. But if you emphasize what you share, resistance and antagonism disappear. With practice, it becomes easy to see yourself in your customers, to align yourself with them. When people identify with each other, they cooperate. So, start cooperating today and you will change the way you sell.

The Greeting

Are you looking for a greeting that separates you from your competition? If so, consider using the following greeting:

"How may I be of service to you today?"

This is an ideal greeting because it's non-threatening and does not lead the customer in any specific direction. When you let people know that you are in the model to provide service, they are more likely to let their guard down and be receptive to your questions.

However, one thing that I have noticed when working with salespeople is some are not comfortable with the word 'service'. If you are uncomfortable with it, feel free to substitute 'assistance' or 'help' with the word 'service'. I strongly recommend that you use the greeting exactly as written. Do not change anything else. The reason for this request will be made clear in Chapter 5.

Determining Needs

As you begin to build rapport with your customer, you will want to initiate a transition from greeting to determining needs. This process can be the result of words or phrases that a customer uses or begun by specific questions that you ask.

As mentioned previously, one thing to keep in mind as you begin the process of determining needs is that the customer has a definite buying process. And part of that buying process is to eliminate you!

Subconsciously, if not consciously, the customer and you are engaged in a battle for control of the selling process. This is the primary source of psychological tension in the selling process. When customers believe they are relinquishing control of the selling process, they begin to feel threatened.

When a customer first walks into your sales office they want control. What follows is your prospect's ideal buying scenario. Give me the prices, let me see the models, and leave me alone. If I like what I see, I'll come back and ask questions. You'll answer those questions and only those questions. Then I'll go home and think about it.

Does that in any way sound familiar to you? I offer this ideal scenario because I want you to understand there is a battle for control when you meet your prospect for the first time. I want you to know that it is okay to let your customer control the selling process initially. When you use the Connecting skills identified in this chapter, control will soon return to you.

The primary benefit of determining needs is that it allows you to build a bridge between your desire to control the selling process and the customer's desire to control it. As you begin fulfilling your customer's needs, you also begin to gain control of the selling process. This is the result of fulfilling your customer's needs through pacing and leading so that they feel satisfied. With each need fulfilled you move closer to establishing rapport. Remember that in new home selling it is okay to follow in order to lead.

The subject of needs is one you can approach directly. Questions involving needs are both professional and appropriate. Customers want to know immediately that your focus is on providing for their needs, and not simply to sell them a home for the sake of a commission.

Some questions, such as financial status, should be approached more discreetly. Examples of questions which help you determine customers' needs might include one of the following:

"Is this something you are considering doing now?"

"What are your reasons for considering buying a new home now?"

"How is your search progressing? Have you visited any new homes that interest you now?"

"What features do you need that you don't already have now?"

The responses to any one of these questions provide you with a transition into a brief discussion of your homes. The concept of transition is fully explained in Chapter 5. Here's an example of how transitioning might work. Focus on the underlined words because those words represent transition opportunities. In the example, also notice that the salesperson is verbal matching by matching the customer's preferred mode of communication.

The salesperson is working with a middle-income family who has outgrown their current home but can't afford an increase in monthly investment. The sales representative's strategy is to have the customer consider a moderately priced single family home that features a small foyer and living room but a larger kitchen, family room and master bedroom.

Salesperson: *"Is this something you are considering doing now?"*

Customer: *"Maybe, we are not quite sure. We have just started to <u>look</u>."*

Salesperson: *"Thank you for <u>looking</u> here; we greatly appreciate the opportunity to <u>show</u> you our homes."*

"What are your reasons for considering a new home now?"

Customer: *"We're renting an older home and the rooms are too <u>small</u>."*

Salesperson: *"What rooms are too <u>small</u>?"*
Customer: *"Our family is <u>growing</u>. Our <u>kitchen</u> does not have space for a table and <u>the family room</u> is too narrow."*

Salesperson: *"Well, I am sure we can solve that concern for you. Room sizes are one of the many reasons people choose a XYZ home. We have studied your concern a great deal, and we have learned that a <u>growing family</u> like yours usually prefers <u>more space in the family room, kitchen and master bedroom</u>. It's a shame to throw away hard-earned money on oversized foyers, living room and secondary bedrooms, when that may not be important to you."*

               "Our belief here is to feature space where you actually spend your time. Let me <u>show</u> you several floor plans that meet your conditions."

The salesperson has learned just enough about the customers' basic needs to enable the customer to focus favorably on XYZ's product. He also has positioned YYZ Homes as knowledgeable, caring and aware of the needs of the market. The salesperson's response also provides a natural transition into more in-depth qualifying questions.

Here are some examples of qualifying question topics: own/rent status, price ranges being considered, number of people living in the household, length of time spent searching for a new home and sense of urgency.

Customers will allow you to ask more personal questions when they are confident that you are genuinely interested in solving their housing needs.

Providing Solutions to Customer Needs

One secret to satisfying your customer's needs is to constantly solve your customers' problems by offering solutions. That is the one thing you and the customer want. You want the sale and your customer wants a solution. It is the primary common ground between you and the prospect during the sale. Establishing common ground is vital to establishing rapport and earning the right to ask for the sale. Solving customers' problems by offering solutions is also the primary source of momentum in the selling process.

Focusing on the customer's real and specific needs must be the thread that runs from the initial meeting through the signing of the contract. The process begins during *Connecting*.

As long as the focus of *Connecting* is to provide service to the customer rather than trying to defeat them in a battle of wills, the customer will not feel threatened. As soon as you stop fulfilling needs (and are therefore demanding more than you are giving), the battle is on and the customers' defenses go up.

As was stated earlier, you cannot usually expect to get too far with the goal of identifying and fulfilling needs in the first minutes of your sales presentation. But you can at least lay the foundation that permits you to naturally transition from *Connecting* to *Discovery*.

Listening

Listening in new home sales is vitally important. It is the cornerstone of effective communication and discovering needs. Most salespeople are not good listeners because they were never taught how to do it, yet the problems this causes affect every level of the selling process.

Listening helps you work more effectively and accurately and makes certain the message you receive is the message your customer means to give. Consider adopting the follow listening habits.

Determine Objectives before Listening

Before you initiate a sales presentation identify what you want to accomplish. The benefit to you is that you remain focused because you have a specific objective in mind. If you know exactly what to listen for, you move toward that objective. When you are listening, you hear what is important to your customer and that helps you sell more precisely.

Take Advantage of Thinking Speed

The average person speaks at a rate of 200 to 250 words per minute. The brain can comprehend up to 600 words per minute. That's a substantial difference. The benefit to you is that you are able to stay ahead of what your customer is saying; especially if you know what to listen for.

In Chapter 5 you will learn that there are only 17 things for which you need to listen. That may sound like a lot but it really isn't. Trust me; your customers give you everything you need to know. You just have not trained yourself to listen for what is important.

Begin now to consider how you can take advantage of your thinking speed.

Avoid or Minimize Distractions

To listen well you must stay focused. You must eliminate distractions. That means turning off cell and office phones when you are working with a customer. It means scheduling one-on-one customer meetings during hours when you know you will not be disturbed. Your customers deserve your full attention. Nothing less is acceptable.

Don't Interrupt the Customer

Patience is a rare commodity among salespeople. But it is a skill worth learning. When you ask a question, prepare yourself to listen for the whole answer. Let your customer complete their thoughts. Let your customers see through your physiology that you are listening intently to their words. Teach yourself to wait until you're sure your customer has finished and then respond. This takes practice because many salespeople like to hear themselves talk. Separate yourself from other salespeople by listening; not talking.

Don't Change the Subject

Stay focused. Your customer came to the model home to determine if what you are selling meets their needs. They did not come to hear about last night's basketball game or your most recent vacation. In our society today, most likely, both spouses work outside the home. Their time is limited and they do not want their valuable time wasted.

In Chapter 2 I asked you to ride the horse in the direction it is going. When you follow that communication principle, I promise your customers will appreciate it. Start today to form listening habits that demonstrate to the customer that you are focused on their needs. When customers feel you are tuned into their needs they begin to drop their defenses and begin to listen to how your product and community can meet those needs.

Understanding the Importance of Time

Time, which once seemed free and elastic, has grown elusive and tight. Our measure of its worth is changing dramatically. Today it is commonplace to shop through catalogs, the television or computer – all done in the name of convenience and time-saving.

For $1,500 you can have a fax machine put in your car, alongside your cellular phone, so people can reach you instantaneously with printed or oral messages. Most salespeople today have a business card displaying a phone number, pager number, E-mail address and fax number.

What has all this gained us? Not more time. You already know there isn't any more. Not more freedom. If you pay someone to pick up your laundry while you stay late at the sales office, your only trading one chore for another. Not more peace of mind. All around you see frazzled parents, exhausted co-workers, and families juggling multiple hectic schedules. As a nation we seem to have run out of time.

And how does this fact 'run out of time' impact you as a new home salesperson? The answer is plenty.

Today's new homebuyer doesn't have adequate time to shop for a new home. According to research conducted by a popular builder magazine, 70% of both spouses are working outside the home. The majority of these jobs are full-time and many require an excess of 40 hours per week. Your new home customers have a limited amount of time to devote to finding and purchasing a home. This is part of the reason your prospect wants to control the selling process. Customers understand that if they are not careful time-wasting salespeople will steal their precious time.

The only way to gain the trust and confidence of your prospect is to demonstrate respect for time.

Develop a Time Strategy

Today's homebuyer uses a process of elimination to decide on which home to purchase. Most customers will visit between six and ten model home communities. Locations are chosen based upon proximity to work, transportation corridors, services, schools, shopping, word of mouth and referrals. New homebuyers also use the newspaper to plan their Saturday and Sunday tour. An increasing number of buyers are making intensive Internet searches to find their new home. In other words your prospective new homebuyers have a definite strategy for maximizing their time. In order to be successful in new home selling today, you must also have a selling strategy to maximize the time your prospect gives you. Your selling strategy begins to form shortly after your greeting with the following question:

"How much time do you have to spend with me today?"

This simple question determines what type of sales presentation you can effectively present that day. If the answer is ten to fifteen minutes (which by the way is the national average for first-time visits) then you know that it will be impossible to conduct a full sales presentation. Your selling strategy must be modified to fit the time constraints placed on you by your prospect.

You might be concerned about asking a question that allows the prospect to control the selling process. Remember the primary benefit of determining needs (and time is a definite need) is that it allows you to build a bridge between you and your prospect. The result is trust and confidence in you. You are actively demonstrating a respect for your prospect's time. You are separating yourself from all other salespeople who may be labeled as time-wasters. Also, remember that it is okay to follow in order to lead.

Customer's today are educated consumers. They have been to other model homes and have heard many sales presentations. Unfortunately, most sales presentations sound alike. You have an opportunity to set yourself apart by being different. When you demonstrate understanding you are building rapport. People want to do business with people they like.

When your prospect provides you with an answer to the question, *"How much time do you have to spend with me today?,"* you must follow the response with your reason for asking the question. Your reason lays the foundation for your selling strategy. Here's an example of how this might work:

Salesperson: *"How much time do you have to spend with me today?"*

Customer: *"Well, I'm not sure. We have several communities we intend to visit today. I guess, fifteen to twenty minutes."*

Salesperson: *"I understand, fifteen to twenty minutes. Let me explain why I asked the question about time. I want to make sure I focus on the things that are important to you. We can discuss our homes, homesites, location, financing, community or builder. What would you like to hear about or see today?"*

Customer: *"Well, let's see, I want to look at your model home, get some pricing and learn a little bit about your financing."*

Salesperson: *"Good. Let's start with the model and then I can show you several of our below rate financing plans. Okay? Let's get started."*

This brief exchange has accomplished several things.

1. You've demonstrated a respect for time.

2. You've demonstrated that you understand what is important and that you will direct your presentation to satisfying those needs.

3. You've established a reason for a second appointment. In Chapter 5 you will learn there are six decision-making categories: community, location, homes, homesite, builder and financing. If you spend fifteen to twenty minutes with the prospect and only cover homes and financing, you're left with four areas to cover either during a follow up call or the next visit.

By using the time strategy you are earning your customer's trust and confidence and separating yourself from all other new home salespeople. The goal of the time strategy is to spend more time with your prospect. Research conducted by the Sales Institute provides this important fact: For every thirty minutes you spend with a prospect your chance for a sale increases by 50%. When you examine the actual time spent with a prospect prior to a sale you learn the following:

1. The number of prospect visits to model home before purchasing is three to four.

2. Actual amount of time spent with prospect before purchasing is four to six hours.

These are national averages and will vary dependent on whether you are selling first-time or move-up customers. But the point is that a sale occurs over an extended period of time. How you set-up the time you spend with your prospect is critical to your success. When you explain to a prospect that there are six key categories to a good housing decision, you are setting-up reasons for additional meetings or a reason to spend more valuable time with you. As you spend time with your prospect and explain the value of your location, community, homes, homesites, builder and financing you are able to gain agreements that earn you the right to ask for the sale.

You must remain constantly aware that a sale takes time. And that each visit to a sales office sets up an opportunity for moving closer to a sale. Each sales encounter provides an opportunity for reaching additional sales objectives. You need to ask yourself the following question after each prospect visit, *"What did I accomplish today?"* The answer sets up how to proceed and will determine what the next step might be.

Overall, you have four objectives to focus on during each sales presentation:

1. Contract

2. Deposit

3. Appointment

4. Phone call

Keep these objectives the focus of your time strategy. The amount of time available will determine what can be accomplished. Time can work for you or against you. It is up to you to manage time successfully. The whole process of managing time successfully begins during the greeting when you ask the question, *"How much time do you have to spend with me, today?"*

The Connecting Process

You only get one opportunity to make a good first impression. How you maximize that opportunity may well determine your success as a new home sales professional. The following summarizes the *Connecting* process, which, if done correctly, will guarantee a good first and lasting impression.

A.   Be on time.

B.   Dress appropriately.

C.   Get up from behind your desk and move forward to greet your customer.

D.   If you're talking on the phone, stand up, smile and acknowledge your customer's presence.

E.   Give your name and get your customer's name.

F.   Use your customer's last name until you establish enough rapport to earn the right to use his, hers or their first names.

G.   Express sincere appreciation for your customer's visit. Remember, customers have choices, let customers know that you appreciate the opportunity they are providing you.

H.   Always offer a firm handshake. Shake the hand, not the fingertips. Gender makes no difference. Make eye contact and square your body to customer.

I.   Respect the customer's space. Four to twelve feet is acceptable social distance. Observe the distance the prospect desires.

J.   Speak with enthusiasm, conviction and confidence about each of the six decision-making categories: homes, home sites, community, location, financing and builder.

K.   Identify with your customer by using anyone or all of the following matching strategies:

    1. Verbal matching – visual, auditory, kinesthetic.

    2. Body matching – static, key gestures.

    3. Minimal cues.

L.   Listen for transitional words that provide you with an indication of why your customer is visiting your model home: job transfer, employment, schools, family, present living standards.

M.   Always follow your customer's lead. Give them what they want and they most likely will give you what you want.

N.   Listen twice as much as you talk.

O. Avoid looking away or acknowledging other customers if already engaged with a customer.

P. Ask permission before greeting new customers. Your customer will never resent your greeting another customer as long as you excuse yourself politely and return in a reasonable amount of time.

Q. Talk with every customer who visits your model home. No matter how busy you may be, there's no excuse for ignoring a visitor.

R. Learn to use elimination questions on busy days to separate the real homebuyers from the shoppers or lukewarm customers. Here are some examples:

> *"Is this something you are considering doing now?"*
>
> *"How soon will you need a new home?"*
>
> *"Are you planning to move to a new home soon?"*
>
> *"Are you shopping for a new home today?"*
>
> *"When are you planning to relocate?"*

Elimination questions do involve some risk and can produce varied results. Even interested customers may be 'turned off' when they're confronted in such a direct manner. So it's best to confine elimination questions to those times when the volume of traffic is high, as when several customers arrive at the same time.

S. Last but not least is to keep a positive frame of mind. Remember that not every prospect is a serious prospect but if you follow the ideas contained in this chapter you will sell more than your fair share.

Final Thoughts about Connecting

The *Connecting* process begins before that first face-to-face meeting with your customer. Your builder has devoted considerable energy and financial resources to assure that your customer's first impression is a positive one. Advertising and promotion, graphics and design, model home parks and displays, all are carefully planned and executed to make a favorable impact on the customer. However, in the final analysis it is you who will parlay the *Connecting* process into a signed contract.

Good luck and good selling!

Chapter 5

Discovery and Qualifying

If you could have three wishes right now, what would you wish? Think about it. A question like that would make the most closed-off person in the world open up. Like most good questions, it's irresistible.

The main reason questions are so effective is that most people are compelled to answer them. Questions stimulate the mind and offer people an opportunity to use their brains constructively. How else can you explain the continued popularity of question-and-answer quiz shows on radio, television, and in recent years, the Internet?

When you ask for your prospects' thoughts and opinions, you give them an opportunity to talk. Most people prefer talking to listening, and when people talk, they give you valuable information. This answering reflex is fundamental to the *Discovery and Qualifying* process that is covered in this chapter. However, it's important to understand the distinct difference between asking discovery questions and asking qualifying questions.

When asking discovery questions, you're asking your customers to share important information, facts that will make it easier to decide if what you are offering satisfies their needs or solves problems they might be experiencing. In other words, discovery questions tell you which conditions you must satisfy in order to make a sale.

When you ask qualifying questions you are uncovering conditions that limit your prospects' ability to purchase. Qualifying questions provide answers to personal information that your prospects may not want to share until you earn their confidence and trust. For years sales trainers have taught that it's okay to ask personal questions immediately upon a prospect's arrival. *Building Results* provides you with a different point of view. It allows you to look at the *Discovery and Qualifying* process from the customer's perspective. Believe me when I say, prospects want to look, compare and evaluate what you are offering before they share their life story.

This chapter will teach you how to transition smoothly from discovery to qualifying questions so that when you ask for personal information it becomes a natural part of the conversation. When you transition smoothly between discovery and qualifying questions, your prospects do not feel you're invading their privacy.

Transitioning is an important skill to learn because it makes your sales presentation seamless and more of a conversation rather than an interrogation. The result is a prospect who feels comfortable sharing important personal information, especially if they're serious about purchasing a new home.

Throughout this chapter you will learn the importance of asking both discovery and qualifying questions. You will learn the importance of repeating to verify what your have heard. You will learn to listen for 'nice to know information' that continues to build rapport and trust. Most importantly, you will learn what new home features and options to demonstrate that earn you the right to ask for the order.

Learning to ask discovery and qualifying questions provides you the needed information to put your customer in the right home and on the right homesite, rather than leaving the sale to chance. The *Discovery and Qualifying* process may be the most important selling skill you learn by reading this book. This is how you learn what is important to your prospect and what may limit their ability to purchase. Without this knowledge, you might as well be flying a big 747 with all the windows blacked out. You know you're flying, but you don't know where. Fully understanding a customer's priorities and limitations helps you 'fly' with a clear vision of your destination. More likely than not you will successfully land exactly where you are supposed to land – on a new home sale.

So buckle up and get ready to look at *Discovery and Qualifying* from a whole new perspective, a process easy for you and, most importantly, welcomed by your prospects.

Asking Precise Discovery Questions

There are certain facts about your customers you must learn and understand, yet you can't ask everything at once. Nor can you risk offending your prospects by asking too many personal questions before you gain their trust. Therefore, you must learn to ask precise questions – friendly in tone yet direct enough to provide the information needed to determine if your customer is serious or simply curious.

Successful salespeople have learned to be more effective, efficient, and to execute a sales presentation better than their peers. They have learned to be more effective by doing the right things with precision and how to execute their sales presentation with consistency.

When you learn to ask precise questions, you become more efficient because a precise question is direct and to the point. Many salespeople waste valuable time with questions that don't uncover prospects' needs and wants but instead focus on the salesperson's needs and wants.

Serious prospects appreciate directness because their time is as valuable as yours, and they want you to know what their priorities are. They also want to know quickly if your product is going to satisfy their needs and wants because if it doesn't, they want to move on to their next housing alternative. Asking precise questions aligns you with your prospects. You learned in Chapter 3 that rapport leads to understanding; understanding leads to influence; and influence leads to the sale. Ask precise questions and you will quickly understand the conditions you must satisfy in order to earn the right to ask for the sale.

Think about a large purchase you recently made; for example, your last new automobile. Prior to visiting dealerships you thought about what features you would like and, more importantly, what features you needed. The features you wanted were negotiable but the features you needed were not. The non-negotiable features you had in your mind represented your personal buying conditions. For example, most likely you had a monthly payment and a style of vehicle in mind. If the salesperson's product met both buying conditions you would have seriously considered making a purchase. However, if the salesperson presented you with a vehicle that was too expensive and it was a SUV, and you wanted a truck you would have moved on to the next dealership. You were not rejecting the salesperson; you were rejecting the solution the salesperson provided because it didn't satisfy the two personal buying conditions you had in mind. When you understand buying conditions you align yourself with your prospect's needs and wants and that leads to a sale.

The Discovery and Qualifying Process

The rest of this chapter illustrates how to ask six discovery and eleven qualifying questions. Amazingly, you only need to uncover prospect information in 17 decision-making or need-to-know areas. Still more amazing, your prospect will provide most of the need-to-know information in his responses. So, an important key to the *Discovery and Qualifying* process is called transitional listening. This is a listening process that will make new home selling easy, fun and rewarding.

The six precise discovery questions help you to understand exactly what conditions are important to your prospect. The eleven qualifying questions help you understand if your prospect has any personal conditions that may limit their ability to purchase. You will learn to ask discovery questions first and then listen for transition opportunities to ask qualifying questions with your prospect's information. This process breaks down walls of resistance because your sales presentation becomes a conversation between two people who have a similar goal – you want to sell a house and your prospect wants to buy a house.

There are two types of precise questions: the open discovery question that stimulates thought and encourages continued conversation and the closed qualifying question that extracts personal information but precludes further discussion. Let's examine the benefits of asking open discovery questions first:

1. They cannot be answered by a simple yes or no.

2. They do not lead your prospect in a specific direction.

3. They improve dialogue by improving responses.

4. They help your prospect discover things that are important.

5. They are used to encourage your prospect to think.

6. They provide answers to your prospects key decision-making conditions.

Let's now look closely at the precise discovery questions you can use to understand your prospects' key decision-making conditions.

In order for new home prospects to make a purchase decision you must gain agreement in six key decision-making categories: home, homesite, community, location, financing and builder. Focus your precise discovery questions around these six key categories. The responses represent your prospect's decision-making conditions; when you're able to satisfy those conditions you move closer to earning the right to ask for the order.

The following precise questions are designed to elicit decision-making conditions. It's important that you ask the question exactly as it is presented. Do not change the wording. In Chapter 2 you learned that words are important and they mean different things to people based upon their past experiences. The precise questions, asked exactly as worded, will compel a meaningful response.

Please understand the importance of exact wording. If you change the wording of the precise question in any way you will change the response you get. Think of these questions as a recipe for success. If you had a recipe for a great tasting chocolate cake, you wouldn't change the ingredients because it would change the taste. That is exactly what will happen if you change the wording of these precise discovery questions. Yes, I am asking you to memorize the questions but believe me; the result will be worth the effort.

The first precise discovery question helps you uncover all the things that are important to your prospect about the home. The first precise discovery question is as follows:

"What is important about the new <u>home</u> we will build for you?"

Now let's take a moment and examine the question.

1. The question begins with the word 'what'. Questions that begin with the word 'what' do not lead your prospect in any specific direction and can not be answered with a simple yes or no.

2. The question includes the word 'important' which causes your prospect to reveal what is important to them. Earlier in this chapter you learned that prospects will negotiate their wants and like-to-haves, but prospects will seldom negotiate what is important to them.

3. The question includes the words 'new home' because you want to remind your prospect there is a difference in homes; some are used and some are new. You want your prospect to focus on the fact that what you're offering is different – it is new – and it has never been used.

4. The question includes a trial close by using the words, 'we will build'. By using those exact words you are eliminating all other housing alternatives – you're assuming that your builder will build their new home.

5. Finally the question focuses on your prospect by ending with the words, 'for you'. It has been said that people tune into their own radio station – WIIFM – What's In It For Me. By using the words 'for you' you tune right into your prospect's very own personal frequency.

Think about it – this first discovery question focuses your prospect on thinking about what is important about the home. It lets your prospect know that you want to understand exactly what you need to provide. Most importantly, it puts your prospect on notice that your sales presentation will focus on their needs rather than your own needs. Believe me those are the ingredients for a successful sales presentation; a sales presentation that earns you the right to ask for the order.

Let's take a look at how this first precise discovery question might work with a prospect.

> **Salesperson:** *"What is important about the new home we will build for you?"*
>
> **Customer:** *"Well, I'm not really sure. We've just started looking. I know we need four bedrooms because we're expecting our third child this fall and we need more space. We also need a larger family room, and, if possible, we want to have separate closets in the master bedroom."*
>
> **Salesperson:** *"Is there anything else?"*
>
> **Customer:** *"Not that I can think of. Well, maybe, if we can afford it, we'd like a three-car garage. My husband's brother recently purchased a new home that has a three-car garage. Even though we probably don't need the extra space, it would be a good investment."*
>
> **Salesperson:** *"Is there anything else?"*
>
> **Customer:** *"Let me think, I'm sure there's something else I'm missing, but I think that covers the things we discussed before I started looking."*

Now, let's examine what buying conditions the salesperson discovered.

1. Needs (non-negotiable conditions) – a fourth bedroom for a growing family.

2. Wants (negotiable conditions) – separate closets in master bedroom.

3. Like-to-have (negotiable conditions) – a three-car garage.

The salesperson has learned quickly what buying conditions must be satisfied and has demonstrated a willingness to understand what is important to the prospect. It only took one precise discovery question asked at the right time and at the right place. Now that is being effective and efficient.

I want to stress again the importance of asking each precise question exactly as it is written. Each has been designed to improve customer dialogue by improving the responses you receive. If you change the wording you'll change the response. So do not change the wording; let the precise question lead you directly to an easier and far more enjoyable sale.

Peeling the Onion

In the example the salesperson used two precise questions: *"What is important about the new home we will build for you"* and *"Is there anything else?"*

The second question, *"Is there anything else?"* is designed to help you 'peel the onion' back and learn more about your prospect's wants and like-to-haves. It's a simple question but very effective because it asks your prospect to think harder.

This question is designed to uncover conditions of which your prospect may not be consciously aware but either wants or would like to have. If you're able to deliver either wants or like-to-haves, you definitely separate yourself from your competition. Most new-home salespeople simply ask one discovery question and begin immediately to pull out brochures that satisfy what they think they heard.

But when you 'peel the onion' back, you discover your prospects' buying motivations. When you understand buying motivations, you've discovered the key that unlocks the doorway to the sale.

Buying Motivations

When you ask the question *"Is there anything else?"* you begin to uncover what is really motivating your prospect to consider a new home. Always remember that your prospect will usually describe the home they want in terms of style, size, price and features. However, what they want to achieve with their homes rarely is apparent.

Ultimately, despite all the facts and features you give your prospect and all the specifications they give you, there will be one or two major motivations that trigger the decision to buy or not to buy. Buying motivations are emotional and difficult for most people to adequately express. It takes careful listening to uncover these buying motivations and correctly interpret them.

There are four primary buying motivations to listen for:

1. Family

2. Investment

3. Convenience

4. Prestige

One or all four of these motivations may be hidden in your prospect's responses. In the example above the salesperson learned the following:

1. The prospect wanted more space – that means the prospect is motivated by convenience.

2. The prospect was expecting a third child – that means the prospect is motivated by family.

3. The prospect considers a three-car garage a good investment – that means the prospect is motivated by investment.

It's important to listen for what motivates your prospect. Purchasing a new home is never easy. The purchase initiates many changes in a person's life and most people avoid changes. By understanding what motivates your prospect, you can begin linking together all the reasons purchasing a new home will make life better. In Chapter 6 you will learn a process for *Building Value* around your prospects' buying motivations. Asking precise discovery questions helps you understand what motivates your prospect, and that's like having a road map to follow that leads you directly to the sale.

More Precise Discovery Questions
The following five other precise discovery questions are designed to help you understand all the other buying conditions you must satisfy before your prospect says, "*Yes*":

What is important about the <u>homesite</u> you select for your new home?

What is important about the <u>community</u> you select for your new home?

What is important about the <u>location</u> you select for your new home?

What is important about the <u>financing</u> you select for your new home?

What is important about the <u>builder</u> you select to build your new home?

The only differences in these five questions are the words homesite, community, location, financing and builder. However, each question provides different information. The responses you get from each question provide you with more and more buying conditions. Clearly understanding your prospect's buying conditions helps you develop a more targeted sales presentation. You're not wasting your prospect's time or your valuable selling time. So, take time now to memorize all six precise discovery questions. Your prospects will appreciate your professionalism and you will appreciate the additional income you will earn.

Timing

You now have learned six precise discovery questions. You may be asking yourself, when do I ask these questions? Do I have to ask them all at once? Is one question more important than another? If I ask each question, is it possible to remember all the buying conditions? Let's take a look at each of these questions and see if I can provide some answers.

When Do I Ask These Questions?

In Chapter 4 you learned to ask your prospect how much time they had to spend with you. You learned to follow up that question by providing a reason you were asking about time. You told your prospect they were going to make six important decisions. They needed to decide on a home, homesite, community, location, financing and builder. You asked them to choose what was most important. Their response told you what precise discovery question to ask first. What follows is an example using what you learned in Chapter 4 and what you're learning in this chapter.

Salesperson: *"How much time do you have to spend with me today?"*

Customer: *"Maybe 15 to 20 minutes. I'm on my lunch hour."*

Salesperson: *"I asked about time because I want to make sure I focus on what's most important to you. We can discuss homes, homesites, community, location, financing or builder. What would you like to hear about or see today?"*

Customer: *"Well, I am rushed for time. I guess I'd like to hear about your homes and pricing."*

Salesperson: *"Okay. Let's focus on your new home and pricing during the time we have. Could you please share with me what is important about the new home we will build for you?"*

That's an example of seamlessly linking two precise questions while following your prospect's agenda. Both you and your prospect win. You learn valuable buying conditions and your prospect learns that you're going to focus on what is important and that differentiates you from your competition.

Do I Have to Ask Them All at Once?

The answer is no. In the previous example the customer let the salesperson know time was limited. The salesperson followed the customer's lead and asked a precise discovery question about the home. Listening carefully to responses, the salesperson begins the discovery process of understanding some of the customer's buying conditions.

By following the customer's agenda and providing information about homes and pricing the salesperson earned the right to ask for a second appointment because the salesperson didn't have enough time to learn about the other five decision-making conditions introduced: homesite, community, location, financing, and builder. ·

Introducing the six decision-making conditions gives your prospect a choice and also provides you with a follow-through opportunity. You'll learn how stay connected to your serious prospects in Chapter 11 by using the remaining decision-making conditions as reasons to call your prospect back.

Is One Question More Important Than Another?

The answer again is no. In order for a prospect to say *"Yes"* when you ask for the order, he must first agree that the home, homesite, community, location, financing and builder satisfy his buying conditions. So, the order of the discovery questions is not that important. It is important, however, to ask each of the discovery questions. Yes, it may take several appointments before you understand everything that is important. But remember, most new home sales occur between the second and fourth visits. Take your time, be patient and learn your prospect's buying conditions. My promise is that you will be rewarded with additional sales and income.

Can I Possibly Remember All the Buying Conditions?

You'll read many times in *Building Results* that one of the keys to successful new home sales is listening. When you ask a precise discovery question you must listen carefully to your prospect's response(s). The words they choose define the value they place on the buying condition. Consider again the following:

1. Like to have – most willing to negotiate

2. Want – somewhat willing to negotiate

3. Need – least willing to negotiate

It is imperative that you listen well and then repeat to verify. When you repeat to verify, you clarify understanding. You are telling your prospect that you will focus your sales presentation on their buying conditions, not yours. Your sales presentation will be targeted and produce excellent results in the limited time your prospects give you. Here's an example of repeating to verify.

Salesperson:	*"What is important about the homesite you select for your new home?"*
Customer:	*"It must have a level back yard and be large enough to accommodate a swimming pool. And I want a north and south sun orientation."*
Salesperson:	*"Is there anything else?"*
Customer:	*"Well, it would be nice if the homesite was located on a quiet street, maybe a cul-de-sac."*

Salesperson:	*"Okay, let me see if I understand. You need a back yard that is level and big enough for a pool. And, it would nice, if I can find a homesite on a quiet cul-de-sac. Is that right?"*
Customer:	*"Yes, that is exactly what we are looking for."*

In this example the salesperson repeated to verify the customer's buying conditions. The salesperson did it to clarify understanding but also to help remember what was heard. It is true that 50% of what we hear is immediately forgotten. When you repeat to verify, you dramatically increase what you remember. So, make sure you ask discovery questions; and be sure you repeat to verify.

Ask Precise Questions Exactly As Written

I want to stress again the importance of asking each precise question exactly as it is written. Each has been designed to improve customer dialogue by improving the responses you receive. If you change the wording, you'll change the response. So do not change the wording; let the precise question lead you directly to an easier and far more enjoyable sale.

Communication Principles

When you ask precise discovery questions you must be consciously aware of two communication principles you learned in Chapter 2. The first is to 'ride the horse in the direction it is going'. I want you to listen carefully to your prospects' answers. If your prospect interprets your question differently than you intended, don't get frustrated or annoyed. Just relax and follow your prospect's lead. The following example demonstrates the point.

Salesperson:	*"What is important about the builder you select to build your new home?"*
Customer:	*"That's a good question. We want three bedrooms, a large family, and a well-appointed kitchen because we both do some gourmet cooking."*
Salesperson:	*"That sounds a lot like our Manchester model. The only difference is that the plan includes a small sitting room off the master suite. Is that something you might like?"*

In the example the salesperson asked about the builder. However, the customer heard the words new home and responded with new home features. The salesperson did exactly the right thing: he followed the customer's lead and rode the horse in the direction it was going. He knows there is still plenty of time to talk about the builder.

Remember, precise questions do not lead the prospect in any specific direction. They are designed to uncover your prospect's key decision-making conditions. When you hear any of the six decision-making conditions, stop what you are doing and listen carefully. You might hear the buying motivation that will earn you the right to ask for the order.

The second communication principle is 'the map is not the territory'. When you ask a precise discovery question your prospect responds with answers that are familiar to him. Remember that prospects talk and decide on buying conditions before they visit a model home. They determine what they want, need and would like to have. Your precise question triggers a response that is consistent with those needs and wants. The following example demonstrates the point.

Salesperson: *"What is important about the new home we will build for you?"*

Customer: *"We need a large family room, and the master bedroom must be on the first floor. Several of the new homes we've toured have that feature, and we like the idea of separating our bedroom from the children. And we want a game room on the second floor so we can watch TV with the kids."*

Salesperson: *"Let me see if I understand. You need a large family room, master bedroom on the first floor, and separate game room for the children. Did I remember everything?"*

Customer: *"Yes, that covers it."*

Salesperson: *"My Wellington floor plan has most of what you are looking for with one exception. The master bedroom is on the second floor. However, it does have the large family room, a second floor game room and one additional feature that you didn't mention. The master bedroom has a large sitting room that easily accommodates several chairs and a large entertainment center for watching TV in the privacy of your own room. And I've saved the best part for last – I have several thousand dollars in promotional dollars I can give you to pay for the stone elevation you wanted. Let's go now and see the house."*

In the example the salesperson asked about the home, and the customer responded with what he considered to be important. The salesperson acknowledged each buying condition by repeating to verify. The salesperson then proceeded to acknowledge that there was a model that had most of what the customer needed and wanted but with one exception – the master bedroom was on the second floor.

The salesperson understands that if he can persuade the customer to visit the inventory home they might be willing to give up the first floor master for a separate and private sitting room. What the salesperson wants to do is change one of the customer's buying conditions by placing them in a new and improved experience. He fully understands that a customer's 'map' changes each time a new home is visited. Yes, it is important to listen carefully, but many times you will not have exactly what your prospect is looking for. When that happens you must place your prospect in new 'territory' (other model homes) so you can effectively change their 'map' (buying conditions).

The great thing about precise discovery questions is that they provide answers to your prospects' key decision-making conditions. Once you understand what is motivating your prospect you can begin building value around what your builder has to offer. Sometimes you have exactly what your prospect has described, but sometimes you don't. When that happens remember the communication principle - the map is not the territory.

Summary

Let's summarize what you've learned so far:

1. There are six discovery and eleven qualifying questions.

2. Responses to either discovery or qualifying questions provide you with decision-making conditions that you must satisfy or need-to-know conditions that may limit a prospect's ability to purchase.

3. There are six precise discovery questions and if you change the wording of any precise question you also change the response you get.

4. 'Peeling the onion' assures that you completely understand what is motivating your prospect.

5. Prospects reveal buying motivations when answering precise discovery questions: family, convenience, investment and prestige.

6. Precise discovery questions can be asked in any order.

7. Follow your prospect's lead; it's okay to show your prospect homes that don't exactly match what you heard and understand.

Begin using precise discovery questions today. You will be amazed at the responses you get. Your customers will appreciate your directness and you will earn their confidence and trust.

Transitional Listening

I've often commented that if I could give salespeople two gifts they would be the ability to ask precise questions and then listen carefully to a customer's response. It is my observation that there is no substitute for these two critical selling skills. The great thing about both skills is that each is easily learned. So far you have learned to ask precise discovery questions now I want you to consider a new selling skill. I call it transitional listening.

Transitional listening allows you to transition smoothly between a prospect's decision-making conditions and their personal information. Your sales presentation becomes a conversation not a confrontation. Unfortunately, most new home salespeople are trained to secure personal information before building trust and rapport. It's no wonder that prospects build walls of resistance between themselves and salespeople. Transitional listening changes that situation by allowing you to build rapport while securing valuable personal information.

The following diagram illustrates the communication cycle between a typical salesperson and customer.

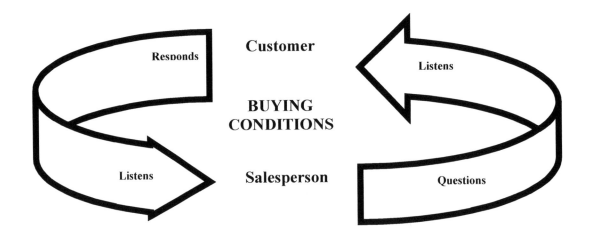

First the salesperson asks a question – then the customer listens, interprets and responds – then the salesperson listens, interprets and then asks another question. This exchange continues until either common ground or understanding is achieved. What I have observed is that during this exchange prospects provide qualifying information that makes achieving common ground easier. The type of qualifying information salespeople might hear includes the following:

1. Visit motivation – the real reason a customer is visiting the model home.

2. Where presently living – location of current residence.

3. Own or rent – whether customer has home to sell or is renting.

4. Family status – the current status of the family.

5. Employment – where customer is presently working.

6. Timing and urgency – time frame for purchasing or moving.

7. Shopping experience – what alternatives are under consideration.

8. Price range – how much house customer can afford.

9. Income – money available to pay monthly mortgage.

10. Initial investment – money available to secure mortgage.

11. Debt – percentage of monthly income already invested.

To demonstrate, consider the following exchange – the transitional opportunities are underlined.

Salesperson: *"What is important about the new home we will build for you?"*

Customer: *"Well, I am not really sure. We have just started looking. I know we need 4 bedrooms because we are expecting our third child this fall and we need more space. We also need a larger family room and, if possible, we want to have separate closets in the master bedroom."*

Salesperson: *"Is there anything else?"*

Customer: *"Not that I can think of. Well, maybe, if we can afford it we would like to have a three-car garage. My husband's brother recently purchased a new home with a three-car garage. Even though we probably don't need the extra space, it would be a good investment."*

Salesperson: *"Is there anything else?"*

Customer: *"Let me think, I am sure there is something else I'm missing but I think that covers the things my husband and I discussed."*

During this brief exchange the customer provided the salesperson four transition opportunities to secure qualifying information:

1. The word *looking* allows the salesperson to transition to a question about shopping *experience*.

2. The word *third child* allows the salesperson to transition to a question about *family status*.

3. The word *afford* allows the salesperson to transition to a question about *price range*.

4. The word *investment* allows the salesperson to transition to a question about *income* or *initial investment*.

Now look at how transitional listening works using the same example:

Salesperson: *"What is important about the new home we will build for you?"*

Customer: *"Well, I am not really sure. We've just started <u>looking</u>. I know we need four bedrooms because we're expecting our <u>third child</u> this fall, and we need more space. We also need a larger family room, and, if possible, we want to have separate closets in the master bedroom."*

Salesperson: *"I see. You mentioned you've just started <u>looking</u>. Are we the first builder you've looked at?"*

Customer: *"No, we toured two other homebuilders yesterday but neither builder offered exactly what we are looking for."*

Salesperson: *"Well, once again, thanks for looking here. I'm sure we can find what you're looking for. You also mentioned that you're expecting your <u>third child</u>. What is your family status?"*

Customer: *"Let's see – it will be my husband and I, our two sons, and of course the baby."*

Salesperson: *"Thanks for sharing that information; it helps me understand your family situation. Other than four bedrooms, a larger family room and, if possible, separate closets in the master bedroom, is there anything else?"*

Customer: *"Not that I can think of. Well, maybe, if we can __afford__ it we would like to have a three-car garage. My husband's brother recently purchased a new home that has a three-car garage. Even though we probably don't need the extra space it would be a good __investment.__"*

Salesperson: *"__Affordability?__ Do you have a price range in mind?"*

Customer: *"Not really. We know we don't want our monthly payment to go over $1,500 per month."*

Salesperson: *"I'm sure that's achievable. You also mentioned __investment__, how much have you and your husband set aside as down payment for your new home?"*

Customer: *"Right now we have $5,000 in savings, and my husband is expecting a $5,000 bonus in the next 30 days."*

Salesperson: *"That's great. You can use either conventional or FHA financing. If you have time today I'll show you the benefits of both financing plans. Other than four bedrooms, larger family, separate closets and, if possible, a three-car garage, is there anything else?"*

Customer: *"Let me think, I'm sure there's something else I'm missing, but I think that covers the things my husband and I discussed."*

Now, examine what information the salesperson has acquired:

Decision-making conditions	Need-to-know conditions
Four bedrooms	Shopping experience
Larger family room	Family status
Separate closets	Price range
Three-car garage	Initial investment

All this information was obtained in a brief conversation because the salesperson knew exactly what to ask and listen for. Transitional listening provides the bridge between your prospects decision-making conditions and the need-to-know conditions that make purchasing a new home possible. Transitional listening makes new home selling easy. All you have to do is ask precise discovery questions and then listen carefully for need-to-know conditions that are included in most customer responses.

My observation is that selling is made more difficult than it needs to be because salespeople don't know exactly what to listen for. Stop now and consider that there are only 17 things you need to listen for. If you take the time now to memorize the 17 decision-making and need-to-know conditions you'll be amazed at how easy new home selling really is. The choice is yours to make, do you want to make new home selling hard or easy? Decide wisely because it's your future you are choosing.

The List
The following identifies both the decision-making and need-to-know conditions. Study and memorize both lists. Then when you meet your prospect for the first time ask a precise discovery question and listen carefully for additional need-to-know questions you can ask based on the information your prospect provides. All the personal information you need-to-know about a prospect is available to you; the key is to ask precise discovery questions first and then listen for need-to-know transition opportunities.

Decision-making conditions
1. Home
2. Homesite
3. Community
4. Location
5. Financing
6. Builder

Need-to-know conditions
1. Visit motivation
2. Where presently living
3. Own or rent
4. Family or living situation
5. Employment
6. Timing and urgency
7. Shopping experience
8. Price range
9. Income
10. Initial investment
11. Debt

Start today using transitional listening during each phase of the sales process. The result will be additional sales, income, and more satisfied prospects.

Asking Precise Qualifying Questions

Let's now examine the benefits of asking precise qualifying questions. These are questions that extract personal information but preclude any further discussion.

1. They extract simple, specific facts about your prospect's personal life.

2. They are useful in gaining commitments.

3. They are useful in gaining feedback during conversations.

4. They can be used to specifically direct the conversation.

5. They can be used to get affirmative answers of agreements.

The following provides you with qualifying questions that uncover all the personal information you need to know about your prospects. All eleven need-to-know areas are covered. Naturally, you'll never be able to ask your customers all these questions at once. Choose the qualifying questions you're comfortable with and make them part of your sales presentation.

Visit Motivation

Understanding your prospects' visit motivation is extremely important. People visit model homes for all sorts of reasons. Some people are curious while others are serious. It is vital that you understand very early in the sales presentation whether you are presenting to a serious or a curious prospect. If you do not understand who you are presenting to you could be wasting valuable selling time. The following precise qualifying question will help you uncover the seriousness of your prospect:

"Is this something you are considering doing now?"

This precise qualifying question helps you understand the purpose of the visit. If your prospect says, "*Yes*" or "*Maybe*" you know you're meeting with a serious prospect. If they say, "*No*", you know you're meeting with a curious prospect. If they say, "*Three to six months*", you know that most likely you're meeting with a serious prospect. The value of this qualifying question is that it provides you with direction. The more direction you have the more apt you are to sell a house. Make this qualifying question a part of every sales presentation and you'll be rewarded with additional sales and income.

Present Residence

The easiest category to investigate with any customer is where they presently are living. Consider using the following qualifying questions to uncover your prospects present living situation:

> *"Where are you living now?"*

> *"Do you live in this area?"*

As you can see each question is direct and to the point. Your prospect will understand your reason for asking. If they live in the area there's no need to discuss all the benefits of your location, they already know the benefits from their daily activities. If they're relocating, they may want you to explain the benefits of living in this location. You win either way. Don't hesitate to ask prospects about their present living situation and reap the rewards of providing good customer service.

Own or Rent

Understanding whether your prospect can purchase now is something you need to know right away. If your prospect currently owns a home, you need to understand what steps, if any, are underway to sell the existing home. The responses you receive to the following questions help you understand if your prospect has any limitations.

> *"Do you own or rent?"*

> *"Is your home on the market?"*

> *"Is it necessary to sell your present home to buy a new one?"*

> *"How is the resale market in your area?"*

> *"Do you have a Realtor?"*

> *"What steps have you taken to sell your home?"*

If your prospect is currently renting, you need to understand if the lease may affect your prospect's ability to purchase. This is an easy category to uncover information because leases can be broken. Most leases have a buy-out clause that is manageable for your prospect. Consider using the following qualifying questions:

"What arrangements must be made with your landlord before you move?"

"Will the lease affect the possession date of your new home?"

"When will your lease expire?"

"Is it necessary for the lease to expire before you move to a new home?"

"Is there a buy-out clause in your lease?"

Family or Living Situation

Never assume a buyer's marital status and/or living situation. Each presents different kinds of status situations that may need to be resolved. Here are a few typical categories:

1. Married without children.

2. Married with children.

3. Single, widowed, separated and divorced with children.

4. Single, widowed, separated and divorced without children

5. Two or more unrelated adults with children.

6. Two or more unrelated adults without children.

Be aware that a potential customer can fall into any category; keep this in mind while qualifying for family status. The following question is the least invasive and consistently gets the best result:

"What is your family or living situation?"

The question is simple, direct and makes no assumption about your prospect's current living situation.

Employment

Your prospect's employment is something you need-to-know early in the sales process. Being unemployed may limit the ability to move the sales process forward. One of the following questions will help you learn about a prospect's profession:

"What is your profession?"

"Who do you work for?"

"Are you currently working?"

"Do you work in the area?"

You will also need-to-know if your prospect is self-employed because of special mortgage requirements to secure a loan. Consider the following questions:

"Are you self-employed?"

"How long have you been self-employed?"

Timing and Urgency

Early in your qualifying conversation with a prospect, probe for clues regarding the urgency of your prospect making a decision and how much time is needed to complete the move. Learn this as quickly as possible so that you can decide what to show and how much time to devote to the prospect. Once again the purpose of this line of questioning is to determine whether your prospect is serious or curious.

The following questions can be used to quickly find out how much time your customer has to reach a decision and how soon the move must be completed. Here are some good examples:

"Is this something you're considering doing now?"

"How soon will you need your new home?"

"How soon would you like to move to a new home?"

"How long have you been seriously looking for a new home?"

Be assured that unless you know your prospect's sense of urgency you may well be wasting valuable time on a prospect that has no intention of purchasing now. Ask any of these qualifying questions and you'll learn quickly if your prospect is serious or curious.

Shopping Experience

This is a category of questioning that many salespeople simply miss all together. That may be a fatal mistake. It's vital that you understand the competition. The best course of action to determine your prospect's shopping experience is to ask direct questions:

"Have you visited any other homebuilders?"

"Are you only considering new homes or have you visited used homes as well?"

"How do XYZ Homes compare in price and value to others you have seen?"

The reason this category of questioning is so important is that you learn first hand who your competition is. If you've done your competition studies you'll be able to build value around the features that you can offer versus the competition. Never forget that people buy on emotion and justify with fact. When you know with whom you are competing, it's easy to provide facts that help people make favorable decisions. Separate from your competition by asking shopping experience questions – you'll be glad you did.

Price Range

Certainly one of the most fundamental qualifying factors – and the most sensitive – is your customer's financial ability to purchase a new home. This is particularly important since most builders cover a wide price range. There's nothing to be gained by showing your customer a home he can't afford.

Probing for financial qualifications is a delicate procedure, especially in the early stages of conversation before a specific property has aroused a prospect's interest.

Approach the subject gently, but don't be afraid of it. Determining a customer's financial ability is basically a matter of obtaining answers in several areas of questioning. These include direct questioning to determine your customer's financial plans and examples that force prospect reaction. Here are some effective questions:

> *"What price range are you considering?"*

> *"XYZ Homes range from $140,000 to $190,000. What price range do you have in mind?"*

Many times your prospect is more concerned about the monthly payment versus the price of the house. If you find that to be the case, consider the following question:

> *"How much monthly payment do you feel will comfortably fit into your housing budget?"*

Often, you can qualify your customer by establishing comparisons. Here are some examples:

> *"Our homes range from $100,000 to $175,000. What price range are you considering?"*

> *"The model you're touring is priced at $175,000. That includes all the finishing details except the furniture and draperies. How does that price range fit into your plans?"*

> *"A minimum investment in these homes would be approximately $15,000 and about $1,400 a month, including taxes and insurance. Does that monthly payment fit into your housing plans?"*

Income

It's important that any possible decision-limiting elements be determined before trying to close. Not earning enough income to qualify for a mortgage limits your prospect's ability to purchase. Therefore, it's imperative that you investigate your prospect's current and future income potential. The question listed below is very direct but this is a qualifying category that requires a straightforward question:

> *"What is your monthly income?"*

It's difficult to ask such a direct question. However, if you've built rapport and trust throughout your sales presentation, you've earned the right to ask direct questions. What follows is an example on how to use transitional listening to ask the income qualifying question:

Salesperson: *"A minimum investment in the home you have previewed would be approximately $15,000. Monthly payment would be approximately $1,400, including taxes and insurance. How does that payment fit into your plans?"*

Customer: *"That sounds a little high. I'm not sure we can afford that much."*

Salesperson: *"I understand. $1,400 per month is a lot of money. You mentioned affordability. Are you familiar with the qualifications that are needed to establish your credit for a mortgage? If not, permit me to briefly review two of the main requirements: debt and income. Let's start with income. What is your monthly income?"*

In this example the salesperson used transitional listening to justify the reason to discuss income. You can do the same thing with any prospect. If he mentions affordability, financing, money or credit, you have the green light to ask about income. Once again, the key to asking very personal questions is to listen carefully and then transition to the delicate categories immediately after your prospect introduces the subject.

When you're working with lower-income customers and those with limited reserves and are seeking minimum terms, explore the specifics of mortgage qualifications relatively early in your interview. Your questioning in such cases might pursue this line:

> *"Since you're interested in using FHA financing, a minimum of $60,000-a-year family income is needed to qualify for the maximum available loan. How does that compare to your present income?"*

Always remember that your prospect understands your need-to-know if they earn enough money to purchase a home. If you ask income qualifying questions with confidence, you'll get the answers you need.

Down Payment

The subject of down payment is not nearly as delicate as income. Questions listed below can help uncover how much, if any, your prospect has set aside for down payment and earnest money:

> *"How much have you set aside for initial investment in a new home?"*

> *"How much equity will you realize from the sale of your present home?"*

Many mortgages today allow your prospect to roll into their mortgage down payment and closing costs. Yes, the monthly payment increases but the advantage is that your prospect can purchase a home with no money down. Take time to study the mortgage business. Learn how the various programs work and become a mortgage consultant to your prospects. The benefit to you is additional sales and income.

Debt

Qualifying your prospect for debt is probably the most difficult need-to-know condition to uncover. Seldom, if ever, will a prospect tell you the truth about what they owe. Debt is a very private and personal thing. If you're selling to financially challenged customers, it may be best to sit down and summarize mortgage requirements so that everyone understands what is involved. Most likely, your prospect will appreciate the education you are providing. Obviously, you wouldn't need to do this if your customer's answers indicated that they are financially capable of meeting minimum requirements of income and debt. Be careful not to put the customer on the spot, direct questioning regarding the customer's financial situation can help. One or more of the following questions can be used:

> *"Are you familiar with the qualifications that are needed to establish your credit for a mortgage? If not, permit me to briefly review income and debt ratios with you."*

> *"Do you mind if I ask you some personal questions about income and debt?"*

Securing information about debt requires trust and confidence. If you haven't built rapport with your prospect, you probably won't be able to ask about debt. My advice is to first build rapport and earn the right to ask the tough personal questions.

Asking Nice-to-Know Questions

So far, you've learned to ask decision-making and need-to-know questions. Now I want you to consider asking questions that uncover what your prospects like to do for relaxation. These questions continue the process of building rapport and trust. They won't lead you directly to the sale but can link what you learn as rationalization and justification for making a purchase decision.

Here are some things that are nice to know about your prospects:

1. Hobbies

2. School preference

3. Church affiliation

4. Shopping preference

5. Athletic interests

6. Other personal and recreational information

Questions you can use to discover your prospect's nice-to-know conditions are as follows:

"Do you have any hobbies?"

"We have two excellent school systems. One is public and the other is private. Do you have a school preference?"

"We have a number of churches close to the community. Would you like me to share that information with you?"

"Our community is located within one mile to the largest mall in the area. Is convenient shopping important to you?"

"We have terrific youth sports programs in this area. Would you like information about the various programs available to you?"

The point is that there are many things about your prospects that are nice-to-know. Knowing these things will not directly lead you to the sale. But knowing what interests your prospects in their daily lives helps you build rapport and trust. Take time to find out what your prospects do during their free time. You may not only make a sale you may make a friend and friends lead to referrals.

The Discovery and Qualifying Process

Most new home sales experts would agree that *Discovery and Qualifying* is the cornerstone of any successful new home salesperson. This chapter has provided you with a better way to discover important factors including those that might limit your prospect's ability to purchase.

Ideas contained in this chapter require study and practice. That's a choice you'll have to make. No one can make that choice for you. I define success as being willing to do what others are not willing to do. If you are willing to take the time to learn the *Discovery and Qualifying* process described in this chapter you will be successful. The following summarizes this process, which, if done correctly, will dramatically increase your sales and income:

A. Ask precise decision-making discovery questions.

1. Home

2. Homesite

3. Community

4. Location

5. Financing

6. Builder

B. Peel the onion to fully understand your prospects' needs, wants and what is important. Remember to ask your follow-up question *"Is there anything else?"*

C. Listen for buying motivations.

       1. Investment

       2. Convenience

       3. Family

       4. Prestige

D.   Repeat to verify information discovered.

E.   Use transitional listening to link discovery and qualifying questions.

F.   Ask precise need-to-know qualifying questions.

       1. Visit motivation

       2. Present residence

       3. Own or rent

       4. Family status

       5. Employment

       6. Timing and urgency

       7. Shopping experience

       8. Price range

       9. Income

      10. Initial investment

      11. Debt

G.   Ask nice-to-know qualifying questions.

    1. Hobbies

    2. School preference

    3. Church affiliation

    4. Shopping preference

    5. Athletic interests

    6. Other personal, recreational information

A Final Word about Discovery and Qualifying

This chapter has listed many questions. No customer is going to let you ask all of them, so you must select questions that meet specific objectives and keep the others in mental reserve for those special situations.

The questions that uncover your prospect's decision-making conditions can not be changed. Each question must be asked exactly as it is written. If you change the question you will change the response. Questions that qualify for need-to-know conditions can be changed to fit the situation. The only thing you can't change is that all eleven need-to-know areas must be explored. Feel free to add questions to each need-to-know category.

If you keep the decision-making and need-to-know categories in mind and practice using them, you'll find that some work better than others. You'll begin your *Discovery and Qualifying* process with questions that produce more answers and thus cover more *Discovery and Qualifying* categories. Always begin each sales presentation with a discovery question followed by a need-to-know question. This demonstrates that you want to follow your customer's agenda. This is a subtle difference but one that your prospects will appreciate.

To simplify the process of gathering information in both the decision making and need-to-know areas, you might consider typing the list of *Discovery and Qualifying* categories as a handy guide. Keep this list of 17 discovery and qualifying questions on your desk to determine what information you've learned and what is left to obtain.

Good luck and good selling!

Chapter 6

Building Value

For years, sales trainers have taught the value of selling product benefits. Books have been written on the importance of presenting features connected to product benefits. If you ask salespeople, and they answer honestly, they will admit that selling benefits is the foundation of demonstrating.

Yet the fact remains, most salespeople don't sell benefits to any significant degree. Why? The reason is based on two assumptions most salespeople make, one partially correct and the other possibly fatal. Let's examine both:

1. First assumption – the customer knows product benefits. This may be true on some products but not all.

2. Second assumption – the fatal assumption is that salespeople assume the customer is thinking about product benefits.

Both assumptions can lessen the impact of your sales presentation. Unless your customer is thinking about benefits during your sales presentation, there is no way he will give proper value to a product feature. And unless he realizes the value of your product, versus the competition, there's no way he can separate you from the competition. Without this critical definition, you're leaving the sale to chance.

Let's begin by taking a look at what goes on in a customer's mind when a purchase as large as a new home is under consideration. It's essential to consider the customer's mental processes, because that's where the buying decision is made. You must influence his thinking if you are to make a sale.

Basically, when a prospect visits your model home he is mentally weighing two things:

1. What do I have to pay?

2. What value do I get for my money?

It's that simple. Your customer is simply asking *"Is it worth the price?"*

To make my point, I'll share an experience I had with a Sacramento builder. At the time I was living in the Midwest, so I decided to fly to Sacramento one day early to accustom myself to the time difference. The builder made arrangements for me to stay at a hotel located across from the state capital.

I prefer staying in hotels with coffee service in the room. Upon arrival I noticed the hotel I was staying in didn't offer that convenience. However, they did offer room service. I checked the price, it seemed reasonable, so I made arrangements to have coffee delivered to my room each morning. The next morning the bellman delivered my coffee right on time. He handed me the bill to sign and I noticed the coffee service was considerably more expensive than advertised. Did I read the room service menu wrong? I decided not to say anything to the bellman. I signed his bill and gave him a tip for providing good service.

My first thought was to read the fine print on the room service menu. Did I miss something? No, I read the menu correctly. How could the hotel charge double what was advertised? Of course I could afford what they were charging but that wasn't the point. I made a purchase decision based on the advertised price. When I considered my purchase I decided that the value I received was not worth the price charged. If I had known the true cost I probably would have made other arrangements.

Your customers are making the same consideration when they ask the question, *"What is the price of this house?"* Buyers want to measure your price against their perception of value. If, in your 'customer's mind', price outweighs value, there's no way you can close the sale because he doesn't think the price justifies the perceived value. The following illustrations demonstrate how price and value might be perceived in your 'customer's mind'. In this illustration the price is perceived to be greater than value received – the result – no sale.

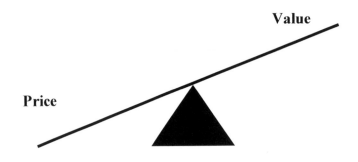

No Sale

If, in your 'customer's mind', price and value are equal, you may get the sale. In the following illustration, at least the customer feels it is a fair exchange – the result – maybe a sale.

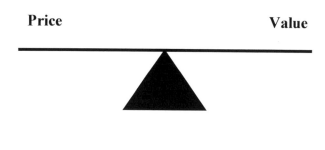

Maybe A Sale

If, however, value outweighs price in your 'customer's mind', that's when you can close the sale. In the following illustration, the home is perceived to be worth more than the price you're asking – the result – a sale.

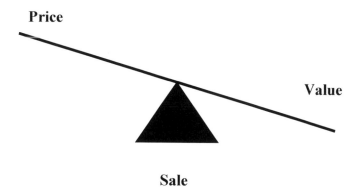

Sale

Please note the key words in the 'customer's mind'. This is important because that's where the value is. Value is nothing more than a measure of how badly the customer wants something. It is a mental thing. That's why you are able to influence it.

A basic principle of your job is to get the value side of the sales scale to outweigh the price side. This brings about one of the great misfortunes in new home selling. The vast majority of salespeople are suffering lower incomes for one big reason – they're simply selling product benefits the wrong way. It truly is a missed opportunity, one that, when taken, leads to more sales and income.

By the way, you may have wondered how my coffee service experienced turned out. The next morning I stopped at the front desk and asked to speak to management. I explained what happened and to my delight the hotel manager removed that morning's coffee service from my bill. He also arranged for my own personal coffee maker and coffee to be sent to my room. Now that is good customer service.

Product Features

Start by dividing the sales scale down the middle. The left-hand side of the scale represents one kind of language, and the right-hand side represents a completely different language. Unfortunately, the majority of people selling new homes are speaking the wrong language.

What's the difference between these two languages? The left-hand language is a manufacturing language. Call it 'product features'. It tells how the product is made, how it's put together and of what it is made. Actually this is where the price originates. It's the accumulation of profit margins, cost of labor, materials, handling, shipping and warehousing – elements that establish a price.

The left-hand side of the scale is important for you to understand. In Chapter 3 you learned that 'knowledge is power'. The knowledge required to convince your prospect to say "Yes" is found in 'product features'. Product features provide the justification for pricing.

When you fail to understand 'product features' you are leaving the sale to chance. Prospects will understand pricing differences from one builder to the next only if they perceive they are receiving greater value for the additional money spent. In Chapter 3, I asked you to secure information about the various products included in your homes. If you haven't done it yet, I urge to complete the assignment now. Understanding 'product features' gives you the knowledge to justify pricing. Don't delay securing information about the various products, do it today.

Product Features

Price

Customer Benefits

The right-hand language on the scale is a selling language, one that few sales representatives speak. It's the easier and more productive language to speak. The right side is called customer benefits, and it is the only language that makes sense to the customer.

In other words, the left side tells you 'how' the product was made, while the right side tells you 'why' the product was made that way. The right side answers the question, what's in it for me, and that is exactly what your customers want to know when they say, "*How much is this house?*"

Customer Benefits
Value

Influencing the Customer's Mind

Since value is in the customer's mind, it's important to understand that value is the only thing you can influence. Thus, as you sell, remember that you can't change the price but you can change the value of the merchandise. Adding value to the scale is what *Building Value* is all about, there's no limit as to how much value you can add. Features give the customer things for which to pay. *Building Value* selling gives the customer reasons to buy. Until your customers have enough reasons to buy, they just simply won't.

Features Justify a Price - Benefits Justify a Purchase

You better decide which one your customer is after. You will spend the rest of your new home selling career either 'justifying price' or 'justifying purchases'. The easier course to additional sales and income is justifying purchases by following the *Building Value* process.

Building Value Process

There are six steps in the *Building Value* process. To work effectively each step must be followed if you want to consistently justify the purchase.

1. Discover needs, wants, what is important and listen carefully for decision-making conditions: home, home site, community, location, financing and builder.

2. State a feature that represents an observable characteristic of the product.

3. Build a bridge by linking the feature to the benefit. Some examples include:

> *"What this means to you is…"*

> *"This will enable you to …"*

> *"This gives you the ability to…"*

4. State a benefit the feature provides.

5. Link feature, bridge and benefit to a buying motivation, such as the real reason your customer is considering a new home. Is it family, convenience, investment, prestige or a combination?

6. Gain agreement through a tie-down question by establishing a value consideration in the mind of your prospect. For best results, ask sensory-based questions:

> *"How does that sound?"*

> *"How does that make you feel?"*

> *"How does that look to you?"*

Here's an example on how the *Building Value* process works. The underlined words identify a separate step in the *Building Value* process.

> *"Here, at XYZ Homes, we include as a standard feature, <u>rear-yard security lights</u> (Feature) mounted under the roof overhang. <u>What this means to you</u> (Bridge) is added <u>safety and security</u> (Benefit). With Jim traveling on business overnight, I'm sure you'll appreciate the <u>security</u> (Buying motivation) that the additional lighting will provide. How does that make you <u>feel</u>? (Tie down)*

Take time to examine the example to understand the selling strategy linked to the *Building Value* process. You'll notice the salesperson learned during *Discovery* that the prospect's husband traveled on business overnight. This fact provided the salesperson an opportunity to demonstrate and build value around one of his builder's many features – rear-yard security lights. The salesperson then links the feature to a buying motivation – family. The salesperson also bridged the feature to the benefit thereby partially justifying the price his builder is charging.

When you understand what your prospects need and want you are able to build value around your builder's many 'product features' by using the *Building Value* process.

A Final Word

Product benefits add no value to the sale unless you bring them to your prospect's attention. Customers are simply not considering product benefits. They are asking themselves: "*Is the home worth the price?*" Your job is to add value to the sales scale, making your customers aware of product benefits by using the six-step *Building Value* process.

To help you better understand the importance of bringing product benefits to the attention of your prospects; consider this experience I had with a Cincinnati builder. I like to role-play during my seminars and, when possible, I like to get on-site with the salespeople. During this particular seminar we were in a model home basement discussing possible demonstration opportunities. I noticed the basement windows were quite a bit different than those most builders provide. The window was vinyl compared to aluminum. It glided side to side which meant it could be opened easily to admit fresh air. There was a safety lock and a screen to keep insects out. I asked one of the salespeople to demonstrate the window using the six step *Building Value* process. The salesperson looked at the window and, with a deer-caught-in-the-headlights look, explained he wasn't familiar with the window.

Stunned, I looked over at the builder and asked if these windows where a new feature. With some frustration he explained that this window was introduced more than a year ago. Because of its many features, I inquired about the price. He said that it cost $128 compared to the $27 he was paying for the cheaper aluminum window. There where five windows in the basement. The builder was paying an additional $500 for basement windows and his salespeople where not demonstrating the value of the better window. That meant his competitor had a $600 or $700 price advantage for no perceivable value. Remember your customers don't know product benefits unless you tell them.

Now before you start to blame the salespeople, please understand that when I asked the builder if he informed the salespeople about the new window, he admitted he hadn't. That doesn't excuse the salespeople, because obviously they hadn't been demonstrating the basement features either.

Hopefully this experience helps you understand the importance of knowing your homes' many features. If you don't know your product, you will not demonstrate it. Always remember that a customer will voluntarily put very little value on the sales scale, that's your job. Until the value side of the scale outweighs the price side, you aren't going to close the sale. It's your responsibility to help your customer understand product values by repeatedly using the *Building Value* process throughout your sales presentation.

Building Value

Before you go onto the next chapter, please complete the following exercise. Select four features in any model you currently build and write a *Building Value* paragraph about the feature using the six-step *Building Value* process. The buying motivation for each feature is included to point you in the right direction.

Then use what you have written with your next prospect. You'll be amazed at how easy it is to build value when you follow these steps. And most importantly, your customer will appreciate that you are building value in the areas important to him.

Good luck and good selling!

Example & Exercise

"Here at (your builder) we include, as a standard feature, <u>rear-yard security lights</u> **(feature)** mounted under the roof overhang. <u>What this means to you</u> **(bridge)** is added <u>safety and security</u> **(benefit)**. With Jim traveling on business overnight, I'm sure you'll appreciate the <u>security</u> **(buying motivation)** that the additional lighting will provide. How does that make you <u>feel</u>? **(Tie down)**

Investment:

_____

_____

_____

_____

_____

Family:

_____

_____

_____

_____

_____

Convenience:

_____

_____

_____

_____

_____

Prestige:

_____

_____

_____

_____

_____

Chapter 7

Demonstrating the Home

What might be considered the heart of the new home sale process – *Demonstrating the Home* – undoubtedly is a key element in the success of a sales program. Many salespeople mistakenly believe this is the make-it or break-it moment. If you've read this book with an open mind, you've begun to understand that there are equally critical parts of the process that come first.

Nevertheless, this is the moment when the buyer meets the kitchen, and the family room, and other important elements of the home.

Three principles to consider about new home demonstrating:

1. Demonstrating is the art of selling features and benefits connected to buying motivations.

2. A good sales presentation doesn't need arguments, it needs demonstrations.

3. You can show more in five minutes than you can tell in one hour.

There is no question that demonstrating is one of the most important links in the selling chain; but if the demonstration is to be effective, you must be aware of its relationship to the rest of the presentation. You also must know how and when it can best be used.

Demonstrating the Home Strategy

Before I discuss the 'how' of the demonstration I want you to consider the 'when'. During my critical path training, I was instructed to demonstrate the features and benefits to every customer who visited the model home. However, after Neuro-Linguistics Programming training, I no longer believe that I must demonstrate the home fully during a customer's initial visit. I've learned that during the initial visit, the customer has a very narrow focus.

When someone visits your model for the first time, they want to look, compare, evaluate, ask questions and possibly eliminate. They don't want you to drone on about the home's many features when they haven't even decided if the home is right for them. During that first visit you must prepare yourself to allow the prospect to tour the model and, when appropriate, begin to build value around the home's features and benefits.

This concept means you must first follow your customer to lead your customer. I know this idea flies in the face of all the new-home sales' critical path training you may have learned, but I want you to really think about what happens when you meet someone for the first time. In Chapter 4 you learned that most prospects are likely to tell you they want to 'look' at the model home. Allow your customer to do just that. Give them time to look and compare. Give them space to explore and evaluate what you offer. Be available to answer questions and offer other floor plans in case your model home doesn't meet their needs and wants.

Adopt this strategy and demonstrating becomes easier, and will be welcomed by your customers. Remember that initially their focus is very narrow, but eventually they need to know everything. Be prepared to tell them everything, not on your timetable but on their timetable. They will appreciate it.

Demonstrating – An Essential Part of the Sales Presentation
Now let's look at the many reasons why demonstrating is such an essential part of the total presentation. Seven key reasons stand out:

1. To establish your credibility through product knowledge.

2. To sell your company and its reputation for quality construction.

3. To explain included features and sell custom features.

4. To ask any remaining discovery and qualifying questions.

5. To lead prospects to minor decisions by utilizing tie-down and trial-close questions.

6. To sell a trip to the homesite, where you and the prospect can look at specific homes or properties.

7. People believe what they see – the most compelling reason of all

Demonstrations are effective because people like a show. They want to see things moving and happening. Thus, you must find the drama and build your demonstration around it. You'll discover that demonstrating makes your presentation more convincing and that, in turn, makes selling easier. That old cliché, a picture is worth a thousand words is especially true here. The real thing is worth two thousand words.

Let's examine the fundamentals of demonstrating in more detail.

Know What to Say

Certainly it's important to know how to demonstrate, but knowing what to demonstrate is equally critical, because it's possible to exhibit the wrong thing at the wrong time. In order to know what to show or say, you must understand the requirements of an effective demonstration. All too often, salespeople appear more intent on justifying their effort than on helping a prospect understand the product presented.

To avoid this and other pitfalls, you should acquire a sound working knowledge of the three basic requirements of a productive demonstration.

Gain a Clear Understanding of Needs and Wants

Know your customers, their likes and dislikes, their needs and wants and their priorities. With a firm understanding, you can tailor each session to their individual requirements. In Chapter 5 you learned that customers come to you with specific decision-making conditions in mind. If you fail to discover what those conditions are, you may demonstrate features of no importance to your prospect at all, thereby wasting everybody's valuable time.

Organize the Presentation Logically

How you organize your material and time your delivery dictate the effectiveness of the demonstration. This really is a show, each part designed to bring the customer closer to purchase. A properly orchestrated demonstration with the appropriately timed elements will have a much better chance of success. Timing is everything.

Early in my career I hired a salesperson who understood the concept of timing perfectly. Throughout the model home he planted sales aids (smaller versions of the actual product) to emphasize his points. They were samples of the product that a customer could pick up, handle and inspect.

For example, he placed blown insulation into a clear plastic bag and stored it in a bedroom drawer. Then when he wanted to demonstrate the energy efficiency of the home, he would take his customer to that spot, give him the bag and explain how insulation works. He helped his customers understand 'R Factors' and enhanced their understanding by allowing them to see and feel the amount of insulation blown into the attic. They walked away with a knowledge and appreciation of the benefits of insulation. He also earned their respect as a salesperson that knew and understood his products.

Look for opportunities in your model home where you can demonstrate the benefits of the elements of your homes. Be creative and don't worry about embarrassing yourself. Remember your prospects want to see your products in action. When you make the effort, you differentiate yourself from the competition and move one step closer to the sale.

Develop an Effective Delivery

Although each individual has a unique style for making a presentation, the salesperson with a forceful, dramatic style keeps the customer's attention longer than the salesperson who simply drones on and on in a boring monotone.

In Chapter 2 you were introduced to an important communication principle – you are always communicating. The demonstration is where you must be particularly mindful of your physiology, voice tones and your selection of the words. Your goal is to get your customer to match your enthusiasm. In many respects you are a performer. Would you rather deliver an Oscar-winning performance or a B-movie performance? Like everything in new home sales, the choice is yours to make. Make the right choice, and sales and income will increase.

Organize the Demonstration

Once you have comprehended the three basic requirements of an effective demonstration, it's time to begin the process of organizing for maximum effectiveness. While there are many ways of accomplishing this goal, four critical elements should be an integral part of every successful demonstration. They are:

1. Customer knowledge

2. Product knowledge

3. Construction knowledge

4. Planning

The following examines each of these critical elements.

Customer Knowledge

This sales principle solves problems through discovery. When you determine your customers' needs and understand their buying motivations, then you can frame pertinent, to-the-point demonstrations to address these needs quickly and efficiently.

The key to discovering customer needs and interests is through the skill of *Discovery and Qualifying* . When you discover and qualify properly, you learn your customer's 'buying motivations' – those special concerns and considerations that can be translated into tailored demonstrations. In other words, demonstrate what is important to your customer, not what is important to you. As a reminder, the four buying motivations to listen for are convenience, family, investment and prestige.

The demonstration also is an ideal time to conclude any discovery and qualifying questions thus far unasked or unanswered. Since few customers enjoy answering question after question before they've seen the product, the demonstration offers an ideal time to complete the *Discovery and Qualifying* process.

Product Knowledge

It is essential to understand the purpose and function of every important home product component and feature. While this is by no means a complete list, the following items should be part of your demonstration package:

Kitchen appliances	Windows	Doors
Kitchen cabinets	Floor coverings	Countertops
Bathroom fixtures	Insulation	Wiring
Lighting fixtures	Water heaters	Heating/AC equipment

A good way to increase your knowledge of these elements is to develop a product manual, an easy-to-assemble notebook containing current product literature. An up-to-date manual increases your product knowledge and serves as an excellent reference when working with customers. One way to gather information is to go to each manufacturer's web site. Product features and benefits are available at the click of a mouse.

Another great idea is to create a notebook for your customers – a kind of home owners' manual. This thoughtful gift brings the highest praise from home buyers for their salesperson.

One final thought on product knowledge. In Chapter 6 you were introduced to a very effective *Building Value* process. There's no better time to use that process than during the home demonstration.

To make my point about building value, I want to share an experience I had with Ryland Homes during one of many customer focus groups I attended. This particular research was conducted on lost prospects. We wanted to know why some buyers visited a Ryland Home but decided to purchase from a competitor.

The moderator asked focus group members why they choose a competitor over Ryland. One said the reason he choose his home over Ryland was quality. He felt the home he purchased was built with higher-quality materials. The moderator asked him to be more specific. He explained that his salesperson had thoroughly demonstrated the home focusing on features and benefits. One feature the salesperson demonstrated was the thickness and sturdiness of the stairway hand rail from the first to the second floor. This impressed him because of a childhood memory of going up to his bedroom, grabbing the hand rail as he flew up the stairs and going airborne! He imagined his own children doing the same thing. When he compared the hand rail in the Ryland home he discovered not only was it thinner but it also was loose.

This experience captured our attention. Quality is a perception. If Ryland was perceived as building an inferior product, clearly that would affect our sales success. We decided to mystery shop the salesperson to learn exactly what he was doing and telling prospects. Armed with this information we could change our product or change our team's sales presentations.

We learned that the salesperson took the mystery shopper on a tour of the model, stopping frequently throughout the house to build product value. When he came to the hand rail he talked about its size and sturdiness. He even asked the mystery shopper to grab the hand rail and give it a good tug to feel its strength. The salesperson was teaching the mystery shopper what to look for and do in other homes they might inspect.

This is exactly what happened when prospects toured the Ryland home. Each prospect grabbed the hand rail and tugged. The hand rail was smaller in size and after being grabbed and tugged by a couple hundred people, it became loose, thus resulting in prospects leaving the model with the perception that Ryland built homes with inferior products which led to poor quality. We immediately changed out the hand rail and eliminated that negative perception.

You can learn many things from this story. First, when you build value in your product, you're teaching people what to look for. Second, by building value in your product, you demonstrate product knowledge. Third, link product benefits to your prospects' buying motivations. Start today to demonstrate and build value in your product – I promise you will not regret it and your prospects will appreciate it.

Construction Knowledge

It's not enough to say that construction quality is good; you have to know how and why, and you should be prepared to demonstrate exactly what you mean. This requires a good basic understanding of construction principles in general.

Many of your customers will have some knowledge of building practices; some will compare your construction quality with the competition. Obviously, it's imperative that you know as much as possible about how your homes are built, because quality construction is one of the selling points you will have to prove. A confident, knowledgeable presentation says more than you realize about you and your product. Think about it. Would you want to buy a high-powered luxury car from a salesperson that couldn't find the engine and didn't know whether it was a six or eight cylinder? I think we both know the answer to that question.

Take time to meet with your builder to discuss your company's building practices. Take notes and be available to work alongside your builder on your days off so you can experience new-home construction first hand. Don't be afraid to ask questions. The construction knowledge you gather will serve as your foundation when you and your customers walk homes under construction.

Planning

It may seem completely superfluous to emphasize this part of the demonstration; yet it's surprising how many salespeople don't plan their presentations properly. Or, unfortunately, don't plan them at all. That's too bad, because carefully planned demonstrations direct your customer's attention to important features and benefits.

Here's how to make your demonstration a real sales tool: Write out the words ahead of time. Mull over the presentation, polish it and shorten it. Work out the words – work in the action. Plan places where you don't say anything.

I am asking you to plan your presentation. I am not asking you to can your presentation. Planning is the key to a good demonstration – be prepared to present what is important to your prospect. That means you have to be prepared to present everything.

Because you may be handing over a huge amount of information; allow it to sink in rather than overwhelming your customers. Most importantly, remember that most people can attend mentally to three-to-five variables at any given time. Therefore, select only the items to demonstrate that satisfy what is most important to your customer.

Rehearse your demonstration over and over. Have your spouse hear it, your sales manager or fellow salespeople. Ask for constructive criticism and don't be upset if you get it. Keep practicing until it feels and sounds right. Remember to include the six step *Building Value* process. Make the demonstration apply to the specific customer. Focus it on the individual, and tell or show how various features will benefit the customer. Fit your home into your customers' needs. Don't ask them to fit their needs into your home. Let the customer handle the product – involve them and let them demonstrate it to themselves. Tie down each benefit as you demonstrate persuading your customer to agree that each feature is important. Keep props and selling aids out of sight until you're ready to use them.

Understand the Principles of Learning
NLP training taught me that when visual and other stimuli are included in the sales presentation, they add realism and facilitate learning on the part of the customer. Specifically, the demonstration aids the use of four principles of learning: participation, association, transfer and insight. Let's examine each principle individually and see how it can be applied to your demonstration situations.

Participation
Learning is an active process. The more your customers are actively engaged in the demonstration, the more they will learn. When a product is tested, the customer has an opportunity to see with his own eyes how the product performs. The more you can get the customer involved with the product, the more likely it is to be sold. An example might be demonstrating a tilt-down window. By demonstrating how easy it is to tilt the window for easy cleaning, you teach your customer the value of the window. Always remember to demonstrate products yourself first and then ask your prospect to participate. This completes the cycle of learning. The great philosopher Confuses said, *"What we hear we forget, what we see we believe, and what we do we understand"*. Get your prospects to participate during the demonstration and they will understand first hand the many features and benefits of your homes.

Association
The idea is to tie-in present experiences with the customer's past experiences. The theory is that the two inputs for thought process are the past (memory) and the present (perception). So the object is for you to use present stimuli to create an association with the prospect's past.

For example, if you have learned through discovery that your customer's fuel bills have been high, it's important to demonstrate the efficiency of the heating system, windows and insulation system. If you have learned that their family is growing and they need more room, demonstrate the sizeable bedrooms, walk-in closets, extra storage, eat-in kitchen, oversized dining room, etc.

To use association effectively, it's critical to learn as much as possible about your customer's background through *Discovery and Qualifying*. Then, you'll be in a position to use the right types of demonstrations to draw on the customer's past to help with the current sale.

Transfer
Transfer is your customer's ability to transfer information contained in the demonstration to actual practice, i.e., to imagine or visualize the use of the product in their own situation. Customers

need to understand how various features will affect them. The effective demonstrator is able to 'transfer' information to the customer and make it seem real. Customers appreciate how features and products will benefit them. A good example of how to transfer information to the customer is to use the following phrases when linking a product feature to a benefit:

> *What this will mean to you ...*
>
> *The benefit to you ...*
>
> *This will enable you to ...*

Using these phrases helps your customer understand how the feature will benefit them. You are personalizing the feature. You are asking your customer to take ownership of the feature. The more you are able to transfer ownership of your products' features, the easier it is to ask for the sale.

Insight

The demonstration also capitalizes on another learning principle – insight. The presentation alone may give the customer relevant details about the home, but it also may be necessary to show the big picture – the total impact and use of the house. In this sense the demonstration acts as the 'clincher' for the sale. It helps you pull into focus all the important points about the product and how they will positively affect your customer's life.

Option Selling

The selling of options during the demonstration presents a special opportunity to provide additional benefits to everyone involved in the sales process: the customer, the builder, and you. Option selling is a positive experience for three reasons:

1. It provides you with a means of tailoring the product to the specific needs of your customer.

2. It enables your customer to customize the home to his exact specifications, thereby, 'personalizing' the house and enhancing its desirability.

3. It improves the profitability of your builder.

It's hard to believe, but some salespeople resist option selling. They consider it a necessary evil to be accomplished as quickly as possible, if at all. In reality, however, option selling constitutes creative salesmanship at its best, because it gives the imaginative salesperson a wide variety of additional tools to help close the sale. Here are some ways to make options work for you.

Know All Your Options

Know all the options, what they are, how they work and what their benefits are. You can't sell what you don't know, so learn how to show or demonstrate each option from the buyer's point of view. Translate features into benefits tied to buying motivations. Emphasize that options will add to the livability and value of the home.

Understand Your Customer's Needs

Make option selling a part of the *Discovery and Qualifying* process. If you know your customers' needs, requirements and financial capabilities, you can weave the subject of options and upgrades into your sales presentation naturally. Most people will automatically want one or more options. For example, they may want upgraded flooring or maybe a fireplace, so work them into discovery as soon as possible.

Limit Number of Options

Don't show all available options at one time. Too many choices may overwhelm or confuse the customer and may create resentment and sales resistance. Instead, program your presentation so that option selling is spread throughout your sales process, a natural part of your presentation.

Add Options to Your Product Manual

Maintain an options section in your product manual. Be sure you have ample information about the products and features you are selling. Customers invariably ask questions and you may not always have ready answers. With a complete product manual, including information on options, you'll have the information you need at your fingertips. Printed material can serve as powerful substantiation of your sales points.

Handling the Option Objection

Overcome objections to options. Some customers dislike the idea of options, feeling they are being 'traded up' or pushed into buying things they don't want or need. Others believe that optional features should be standard. It's important to stress the benefits of a well-designed options program – the ability to buy only the options and upgrades the customer wants. Point out the economy of volume production and the opportunity to personalize the home for individual tastes.

Probably the biggest advantage of an options program is a homebuyer's ability to create an environment personalized to his or her specific lifestyle. It is their privilege and responsibility to decide which options they want and can afford. And it's this freedom of choice that makes them feel that their new home will be built exclusively for them.

Demonstrating the Home Process

Demonstrating the Home is an art as well as a process. The following outlines ideas taught in this chapter. Follow this process to simplify the new home selling process for yourself and insure that the process is entertaining and enlightening for your prospects.

A. Begin at the front of the house. Never start your demonstration by walking directly from the sales office to the model.

B. Remember to use the six-step *Building Value* process, always linking product features to benefits. Your customer definitely wants to know "What's in it for me".

    1. Discover what is important.

    2. State a feature.

    3. Build the bridge between feature and benefit

    4. State a benefit.

    5. Link feature to buying motivation.

    6. Gain agreement by utilizing tie-down.

C. Build value as you walk to the front door by focusing on the uniqueness of community streetscapes.

D. Continue to build value in your product by highlighting several architectural details included in your model's exterior.

E. Open the front door, step aside, and allow your prospect to look, compare, evaluate and ask you questions. Let your prospect experience the house before you start demonstrating.

F.   When appropriate, build value in interior product features by utilizing the six- step *Building Value* process.

G.   Focus product demonstrations on the decision-making conditions in the *Discovery and Qualifying* process. Limit your product demonstrations to what your prospect can absorb. Most people are limited to three-to-five variables at a time.

H.   Involve your prospect in the demonstration. What people do, they understand.

I.   Use trail closes and tie-downs to get prospect to make minor decisions or to gain agreement.

J.   Continue to ask remaining unanswered discovery and qualifying questions during the demonstration.

K.   Personalize the home by demonstrating options that make the home a one-of-a-kind design.

L.   Begin to transition from *Demonstrating the Home* to *Demonstrating the Homesite*.

Final Thoughts about Demonstrating

Probably the most significant thing to remember about the art of demonstrating is to link features to benefits and then to buying motivations. Merely mentioning the features in a home will not be enough to convince your prospects to buy. They must know what a feature will do for them, so it's to your advantage to study all of your products' features and then translate them into benefits that a potential buyer will understand and can relate to based on their own needs.

Always demonstrate those features and benefits that are particularly appealing and outstanding to your customers, especially those which the competition does not have and those you know will press their buying motivations.

Demonstrating can be one of the most rewarding and enjoyable aspects of new home selling. But it's like any communication skill – it must be polished and sharpened before its true potential can be realized.

Good luck and good selling!

Chapter 8

Demonstrating the Homesite

Second only to the home, its construction, quality and design is the homesite. You've heard the old real estate cliché 'location, location, location'? Well, here's where you get to talk about location within the community, within the school district, within the neighborhood.

How do you feel about homesites? Do you think of them merely as convenient places to put houses, perhaps as necessary but bothersome details that complicate the selling process? Or do you view them as opportunities, indispensable aids on the way to the sale?

In fact, a thorough knowledge, understanding and appreciation of homesites are prerequisites to success. You won't close many new-home customers if you're unable or unwilling to demonstrate the site.

To enhance your homesite selling ability, keep these fundamental principles in mind:

1. Every homesite is unique.

2. Every homesite is different.

3. No two are alike.

Each time you demonstrate a homesite, you are showing a product that is exclusive and irreplaceable. You're offering your customer an opportunity to own something that no one else may own. Each homesite is one-of-a-kind, the only one like it in the entire world. This is the kind of thing buyers love to hear. They are looking at a home, a site and a neighborhood that will provide the environment they perceive as ideal and perhaps even unique for their family's needs.

This exclusivity constitutes a powerful selling force. The late Rosser Reeves, who headed one of the world's largest advertising agencies, BBD&O, called this force Unique Selling Proposition or USP. He claimed that every worthy product embodied a unique characteristic, a special quality that made it desirable. He is quoted as saying, *"Discover that quality, define the product's USP and people will buy"*. In the case of homesites, the USP is exclusivity and that's a compelling reason to buy. But you must back your USP with personal knowledge.

Production's Point of View

The decision to build a certain home on a particular homesite is made by the production and land department in a carefully considered decision involving many factors: drainage, easements, codes, aesthetic considerations, profitability.

Regardless of the type of homesite, land-planners must consider other factors, they are:

1. Slope and drainage – this may be the most important consideration since an error in drainage design can be difficult and costly to rectify, often resulting in an unhappy customer.

2. Setback – this is the distance a house sits back from the street. Minimum setback is the goal, since it reduces the cost of concrete for driveways and the cost of sewer and water lines, etc. However, staggered setbacks may be required because of code or aesthetic reasons.

3. Restrictions – easements, rights of way, septic locations and sideline requirements are major restrictions, all of which will affect the siting of a house.

4. Trees – wooded lots add to the beauty and salability of a home, yet they pose special problems for a builder. Trees can cause drainage problems if they inhibit grading. They often are difficult to save, so check with your builder to understand the policy on trees. Keep in mind that it's better to remove and replace a tree than to risk having the tree die, an event that results in a very unhappy customer.

5. Fill – location of fill is important to the siting decision, as is the amount required. Obviously, the more fill that is needed, the more expensive the homesite will be to develop.

6. Sewer elevation – this is an obvious consideration, especially with low side lots where sewage flow may be a problem.

These are a few of the factors that must be considered before a house is sited. They are issues you should understand so you can frame intelligent responses to your customers' questions. Most importantly, each homesite will take only a certain type of house. Yet many customers will want a certain homesite but will not be happy with the house that has been selected for it. If you help the buyer understand why a siting decision was made, you are one step closer to the sale.

Perhaps the best way to learn is to meet with your builder, walk some lots with him and learn the different lot types. See first-hand what the problems are and how they affect siting decisions.

Then, make it a practice to analyze homesites on your own. Put yourself in production's shoes. Think like a builder. Select a group of homesites and prepare your own siting survey for each. Finally, compare your hypothetical decisions with the homesite list. With a little practice you'll find that your analysis will consistently agree with productions. It's a useful exercise that will increase your knowledge and understanding of the siting process.

Customer's Point of View

Once you understand the rules of siting, you can begin to match your inventory of homesites with your customers' requests. This implies an in-depth knowledge of the homesite list. It assumes that you know which sites are available and the houses that may be built on them. And it assures your information of always being current, accurate and up-to-date. Without this knowledge, you're at a serious disadvantage; you will not be able to serve your customers effectively. However, timely intelligence will prepare you to guide your customers to precisely the right homesite.

Use Your Homesite List Creatively

As you begin each sales day, review your products. Study your homesite list and select your key lots. Decide which homesites represent the best value and which ones you would most like to sell today. Picture homes on the lots, and review their benefits in terms of price, view, sun orientation and amenities.

Choose Alternatives

It's best to select at least two homesites for each home you have to sell. Determine possible reasons for choosing one over the other in terms of benefits. This gives you the advantage of helping your customer make a choice, which in turn helps him reach a decision.

Offer a Real Comparison

As you make selections from the available inventory, pick an alternative site, which achieves a true comparison. If you have two homesites available for the same style, select the two least similar in benefits. Then, when you begin the selection process with the customer, begin with the less likely of the two. In other words, sell the lesser lot first. If they like it and buy it, you'll still have the one with more benefits available for the next customer. If it's not at all what they have in mind, you can easily upgrade to the better one.

There is, of course, another benefit to this: it prevents you from being left with only the tough lots to sell when the community is nearly sold out.

Narrow the Selection

A buyer can't select from ten properties any more than he can from one hundred. You must narrow the choice down to one or two as quickly as possible. Otherwise you just confuse the issue and give your customer a chance to 'think it over', which could result in losing the sale. Don't give your customer too many choices.

Therefore, the first person to make a decision must be you. If you can't decide which properties to present, to demonstrate and sell, you can't expect your customers to make a decision. Your daily preparedness and your personal enthusiasm for what you have to sell will help your prospects make the right decision.

Put Your Customer on the Homesite

There is a point along the selling path where friendly yet persistent persuasion is a must. You simply will not sell houses unless you get buyers out of the models and onto your homesites. Thus you need convincing reasons why your prospects should go out and look at specific homesites that meet their decision-making conditions.

Ask them point blank. Through effective communication, inform your prospects that you have a homesite that's exactly what they're looking for, and now is the time to visit.

> Salesperson: *"I have a homesite on Clareknoll Court with a huge back yard and nestled in a cul-de-sac. The benefit to you is less traffic – ideal for your kids. Let's go take a look at it now, okay?"*

If they're in a hurry, tell them it will take very little time. Make a promise that they can be out and back in a few minutes:

> Salesperson: *"Folks, you're here now, and we can be out and back in just a few minutes. I really think you should see it now."*

Show them a picture. If they give you a firm 'no' in either of the preceding examples, back off a bit or set another appointment. However, if the 'no' was not quite so firm, show a picture of the site or the location on the map to spur interest.

> Salesperson: *"Jan and John, this is a picture of the homesite I'm talking about. Rather than make you come back at another time, why don't we have a look right now? You're already here, and we'll be out and back in a few minutes. Then you can get an idea of what it's like, and we can set another time for you to look at it more closely. What do you say?"*

Have them follow you. If they're still saying *"No"*, suggest that they take their car and follow you to the site for a quick look.

> Salesperson: *"Tell you what, why don't you follow me to the site. Then, after a quick look, you can leave from there. Okay?"*

Always keep in mind that your impression should guide you as to just how far you can push your prospects with 'persistent persuasion'. You should push just as hard as you can without becoming overbearing, because you know from experience that if the customer leaves without becoming 'emotionally involved' with a particular property, there's a good chance your competitor down the road might get a grip on them and never let go.

I also know from experience that people aren't always truthful and often try to mislead you. A potential buyer can sometimes 'outsell' a salesperson with the simple statement:

Customer: *"We're in a hurry right now, but we'll come back soon"*

Learn to defeat this elimination strategy by having a planned answer ready, one which includes some tempting reasons for the customer to spare just a little more time. Often, this can make all the difference. Above all, never finish a presentation without saying, *"Let's go look at homesites."*

Demonstrate with Style and Showmanship

When you demonstrate homesites, do it with a dash of flair and imagination. Many customers won't be able to visualize how a house will look on a homesite – they'll see only an empty piece of land – so it's up to you to paint a vivid verbal picture of how the completed home will appear.

What you want to do is build the house in your prospect's imagination. You want to 'move them in' by creating a finished home in their minds. Use your physiology, tonality and well-chosen words to create a home they can visualize as their own.

Demonstrating the homesite is a formidable challenge, and it's also one of the most creative facets of selling. Do it well, and you'll immediately begin to see additional sales and income. Repeat and referral business constitute the majority of sales by most top producers, and it all began with great service at the beginning of their careers. Putting customers on the right homesite is one of the best services you can provide.

If you know that a customer is interested in a particular model, consult your homesite list and select the one site you think is best. If possible, stake off the house ahead of time, learn where the garage and driveway will be, and where other amenities such as decks and patios will be located. This preparation will demonstrate your professionalism and knowledge.

Make Sure Your Homesites Look Buyable

Keep your homesites presentable. Pick up trash and debris. Make sure your prospects can safely walk the homesite lines. See that the 'homesite available' sign is clean and properly placed. Be consistent when placing available and sold signs. Pick a setback from the curb and stick with it.

Ask your builder to help you; after all, it is in his best interest to maintain clean homesites. Also, keep your sites mowed during spring and summer months. This is normally a responsibility of the developer and builder, but you can easily remind them of lot maintenance issues through phone calls, e-mails and meetings.

Obtain the Right Props

To demonstrate homesites effectively and efficiently, you'll need to acquire a few props. Keep them in the trunk of your car so that they're always readily available to you.

1. Several pairs of inexpensive boots in a range of sizes for when the going gets muddy. Boots are available for about $10 to $25 a pair from a number of sources.

2. At least two if not three umbrellas. Look for big, inexpensive golf umbrellas at discount stores. Put them everywhere – in your car, in the sales office, at models. If you only use them two or three times a year, it will be worth it.

3. At least four rain parkas. Check out dollar stores and buy enough to give them to your customers and their kids. Better yet, have them imprinted with your builder's logo! Great visual advertising for years to come.

4. Wooden stakes or plastic tent pegs to identify the lot corners.

5. A ball of heavy twine or cord to connect the stakes.

6. A 100-foot measuring tape. (A great giveaway is an inexpensive tape measure with your builder's logo.)

7. A compass to identify which direction the house will face.

8. A plat map showing lot size, easements and sun orientation. This is the kind of thing that gets your prospective buyers involved and turns them into confirmed buyers.

9. A three-ring binder to hold floor plans and other printed material you may need to refer to on the homesite.

10. Sold signs. Let the buyers plant the sign.

11. Digital camera. Take a picture of your buyers planting the sold sign. E-mail them a copy, or better yet print a copy to give them. Instant camera

and printing technology is advancing so fast, this is an easy gesture that translates to that extra service differentiating you from the competition.

Keep a Plat Map Updated

To demonstrate your community knowledge, keep your plat map updated by listing the name of all existing homebuyers by homesite. Include ages of children, if applicable. List the type of house purchased on each homesite including elevation, and garage location. List the brick, siding, or stone color of each house. Identify special features of homesite: trees, green space, easements, additional depth or width, setbacks, sun orientation and other unique characteristics. Once on the homesite ask your prospect to hold the plat map while you discuss all the collected information that pertains to the homesite.

Physically Involve Your Customers

Use your tape measure; walk the homesite boundary lines, or pace off the dimensions of important rooms or amenities. The name of the game is participation, both physical and emotional, so use your imagination to complete that mental picture. The more your customers become involved with the homesite, the more they're can imagine themselves living on the homesite and the easier the close will be.

Give your imagination free rein. Think of ways to add a healthy helping of participation to your presentations. It isn't easy selling a house that doesn't exist on a piece of land that hasn't been improved, but creative selling principles that are both imaginative and innovative can do wonders.

Demonstrating the Homesite Process

Demonstrating the Homesite is the one step in the *Building Results* selling process that can differentiate you from other sales people. Most of the salespeople you compete with will meet, greet, qualify and demonstrate the home, but very few will *Demonstrate the Homesite*.

Prove it to yourself; go across town (where other salespeople don't know you) and mystery shop the competition. See for yourself that *Demonstrating the Homesite* is not for everyone. Therefore, use *Demonstrating the Homesite* as your big selling advantage. Make sure you touch all the bases by using the following process to stay on track to new home sales success.

1. Walk all your homesites with your builder. Ask questions about how the house will be sited. Take notes and then commit to memory what you have learned.

2. Secure an up-to-date plat map. Identify each home sold and under construction. List names of purchasers, style of home purchased, brick and siding color and names and ages of children.

3. Identify the USP's (sun orientation, trees, open space, extra width or depth) for each homesite and include on the plat map.

4. Put together a 'tool box' of props (tape measure, compass, sold signs, digital camera, etc) and place it in the trunk of your car.

5. Ask every prospect to look at homesites (no exceptions).

6. If possible, take the prospect in your car. While driving to the homesite, sell the many neighborhood values by using the *Building Value* process you learned in Chapter 6. Always remember to help your customers determine 'What's In It For Me'.

7. Physically involve the prospect by walking the homesite rather than viewing the homesite from your car. In Chapter 3 you learned that the 'map is not the territory.' When you physically put a prospect on the homesite, you change their 'map' forever because you put them in a new experience.

8. Build value around all the USP's you identified for this one-of-a-kind homesite by utilizing the six-step *Building Value* process.

9. Ask for the order. Think about it, you've done all the work. You've connected and discovered, and now you understand your prospects decision-making conditions. You built value in the home, community, location, homesite and builder, and now it's time to close. The worst thing that can happen is your prospect says "*No*". And that's a good thing because with every "*No*" comes a reason why. You didn't fail – your solution failed. Stay positive and move on to the next homesite.

Final Thoughts about Demonstrating the Homesite

Tom Richey is quoted as saying, "*Get your customers to the homesite and you will write*". My experience supports that truism. Too many salespeople fail to earn their customer's business because they eliminate this important step in the selling process.

Too many salespeople hand their customers a plat map and point them in the right direction. This is a fatal mistake. If you want to separate yourself from the competition, learn how to demonstrate the homesite. I promise if you commit to *Demonstrating the Homesite* consistently, your sales and income will increase. Like so many of the selling skills I've discussed throughout this book, the choice is yours to make. Make the right choice and begin *Demonstrating the Homesite* today.

Good luck and good selling!

Chapter 9

Handling Resistance

If there is one consistent theme in new home sales, it is homebuyer resistance. In fact, if you don't experience homebuyer resistance, more than likely you won't get the sale. Therefore, welcome resistance because it's a crucial part of the home buying process and quite often helps uncover the solution that motivates prospects to become homebuyers.

Homebuyer resistance generally falls into two categories: misunderstandings and drawbacks. Misunderstanding is usually the result of a customer lacking information or being misinformed about a particular feature or benefit. Drawback is usually the result of either your product failing to provide a benefit the customer considers important or the customer simply not liking something about your homes.

The misunderstandings and drawbacks you encounter become 'stumbling blocks' or 'stepping stones', depending on how you handle them. The real sales professionals in our business have sharpened their communicative skills so they can manage their customers while smoothly negotiating the hurdles created by misunderstandings and drawbacks.

Let's take a closer look at how you can work effectively with both misunderstandings and drawbacks.

What Is Resistance?

When you first hear a comment that sounds like resistance, remember that it may not be resistance at all. There are at least four other possibilities:

1. A mere comment with no real significance.

2. A request for additional information.

3. A buying signal that indicates mounting interest.

4. A real issue which must be resolved at the right time.

When you first encounter resistance you can seldom be sure which of these four possibilities actually are involved, but you will know how to handle the resistance by following the *Handling Resistance* process revealed in this chapter. Before I reveal the actual process, let's examine the four possibilities to see if they sound familiar to you.

The Mere Comment

In the process of trying to think through the complexities of housing decisions, homebuyers often feel the need to talk out their formative thoughts before these comments become actual conclusions. This is particularly true of prospects that have extroverted personalities. Many times this personality type thinks out loud. What you are hearing is their thoughts, not necessarily an objection. Take the information you hear, retain it and act on it if necessary.

As a new home salesperson, one of your primary roles is to act as a sounding board for your prospective homebuyers. You will help your customers express their thoughts without getting in the way. For example, you are showing a home to a couple and the wife remarks, *"My, this bedroom is small."*

Now, that doesn't necessarily mean she doesn't like the house. It could be a sincere reaction but possibly is only a minor point. She might have been thinking about her furniture and how it would fit. Or, she could be comparing the room to another model home recently toured. In any case, when this resistance is first introduced, you don't know what she means. Therefore, treat it gently – if at all.

A Request for Information

When a customer first raises an objection, the facts to counter it are not presented. The customer usually has insufficient information at this time, and it is up to you to judge when to present additional data. Sometimes it is wise to briefly cover the matter then, or it may be best to wait. You might respond:

> *"I have information in my office that will explain the energy efficiency of our windows. I'll include that information in your brochure package or we can go back to my office now. Which do you prefer?"*

Remember, timing is everything. You are the only one in the experience so it is always going to be your decision to wait or answer. When you give your customer the option to discuss it now or wait, most likely, they will choose to wait but at least they know it was their choice. The benefit to you is added trust, and you are given more time to consider a well-thought out response.

Buying Signals

If you review past sales, you'll discover that few, if any, were completed without at least one or more serious misunderstandings or drawbacks being introduced. Customers who are sincerely interested invariably will have things to talk about which may sound like objections. That's because they are more than passively interested in your house. These drawbacks or misunderstandings are, in fact, often 'buying signals'. Purchasing a home is always a big step, and it usually generates inner conflicts and self doubts. The natural instinct is to toss out obstacles to slow the onrushing conclusion. Be sensitive to resistance which may be buying signals. They may be your clue to start closing.

A Real Problem

Sometimes, of course, your customers will raise real objections which must be resolved if the sale is to be completed. While there's no instant formula for making you an expert on handling resistance, there is a six-step process that aligns you with your customer so a good decision can be made. The following six steps provide you with common sense how-to strategies for handling customer resistance:

1. Agree

2. Pause

3. Question

4. Verify

5. Reframe

6. Tie down

Now, let's take a closer look at each step.

Agree

Agreeing is simply an acknowledgment that you heard what your customer said. An agreement can simply be a nod of the head, the word 'okay' or maybe a statement, such as; 'I appreciate your concern'. The purpose of the agreement is to demonstrate to the customer that you are listening and are aware of the resistance. The agreement is designed to give you time to think about how to respond. In reality, it is a stall.

There are three other ways to agree, you can:

1. Agree with the truth – what the customer is saying is true.

2. Agree with the odds – what the customer is saying may be, could be or possibly is true.

3. Agree with the principle – what the customer is saying makes sense in general.

Any of these create confusion in the mind of the customer. They will expect you to defend your position against their resistance. When you agree with the truth, the odds or the principle, you demonstrate understanding. Remember, by agreeing you've aligned yourself with your customer because you're looking at the misunderstanding or drawback from their perspective, not yours.

Agreement moves you toward the customer rather than away. Throughout the new home buying process you must continually look for opportunities to align yourself with your customer. Maintaining balance between you and your prospects is one of the hallmarks of the true new home sales professional.

Consider handling resistance by following the thoughts contained in this short poem:

> *If I see John Smith through John Smith's eyes,*
> *I'll sell John Smith what John Smith buys.*

Once you practice the concept of seeing through your customer's eyes you'll be amazed at how fast the wall of customer resistance comes tumbling down.

Pause

After you agree, simply pause. Do not say or add anything to your agreement. Be still and quiet. Allow your customer time to mentally process that you are agreeing, not defending or arguing. In some instances a customer's resistance may melt away because nothing can be done about the objection. It is what it is.

Pausing takes practice and patience. The act of saying nothing is difficult to do. Your natural inclination is to provide reasons for your customer to move forward but resist that tendency. Allow your customers time to consider the objection and decide whether it's something with which they can live. By pausing, you've tossed the objection back to them, implying they should 'make a decision'.

Often your customer will verbalize acceptance or demonstrate through non-verbal means acceptance. If you witness either verbal or non-verbal acceptance continue with your sales presentation, congratulations, you've handled the misunderstanding or drawback.

Question

If you recognize that the resistance is not going to go away, then move to the next step. First, clarify resistance through questions. Ask yourself, *"What exactly is the misunderstanding or drawback?"*

Is it a simply a misunderstanding or something more serious such as a drawback? You can't overcome resistance until you know what it is. Go beyond the words and be sure you understand what's keeping your customer from making a decision.

In Chapter 5 you learned how to 'peel the onion'. You may have to use what you learned because until you fully understand what is holding your customer back, you won't be able to offer a solution. What follows are the benefits you gain from truly understanding your customer's resistance.

1. Demonstrates that you take the resistance seriously.

2. Targets your customers' real concerns.

3. Reassures your customers they are making the right decision. Resistance often is based on fear of making a commitment that might be regretted later.

4. Allows customers to become less defensive and reveal their real resistance. When they see you are trying hard to understand their resistance, many

will tell you what they really think or even admit the issue is a rationalization for an underlying fear.

5. Gains you time to prepare an answer. By clarifying the issue through questions, you answer more thoughtfully instead of shooting from the hip.

Clarify the Resistance

The best way to clarify resistance is to restate the resistance as a question – then pause for your customer's reactions. Here are some examples of how it might sound:

> *"You think the risks are too great. Is that it, Mr. Jones?"*

> *"You believe the interest rate is higher than you'd pay to our competitor. Is that your concern?"*

> *"You seem to be saying the house is too small for your family. Is that your concern?"*

Go beyond the stated issue to the underlying resistance – don't just restate the words you hear; reflect on what you think these words really mean.

Communicate respect for the issue – never imply directly or indirectly that the issue is foolish or that the customer doesn't have a right to his feelings. Sympathize and empathize. When customers feel they aren't challenged, they relax and become more receptive.

If you're unsure of the real issue, ask questions – prospects don't mind your questions.

> *"I'm not sure I understand your real concern. Could you tell me so I don't make the wrong assumption?"*

Continue clarifying as you answer and close – look for reactions to your answers and to your requests for the order; they may reveal that you did not understand the objection. If so, back up, apologize for not understanding, clarify again and give another answer. Your physiology, tonality, and word selection are as important as your questions. Demonstrate your desire to understand through words, actions, and voice inflection.

Classify the Resistance

Classifying resistance helps you determine the best way to respond. There are seven different classifications. The following identifies and explains each classification:

1. Stall – a stall is any reason given to postpone action.

    "I want to think it over."

    "I have to discuss it with my wife (lawyer) (husband) (parents)."

    "I'll call you back."

    These are classic stalls. Some are legitimate but most are simply rationalizations. Because some people fear commitment, they cover their fears with plausible but insincere stalls.

2. Doubt – doubt indicates a lack of confidence in you, your company or your product. Your customer is questioning whether the home will do what you say it will, whether the builder will provide promised services or whether you have the ability and motivation to solve their problem.

3. Request for reassurance – the prospect wants reassurance that they aren't making a mistake, that you sincerely care about their welfare, and that you and your company will continue to provide good service after the closing. Listen carefully to what they say. Are they asking for information to clear up a misunderstanding, or do they need proof or reassurance? Once you decide it's reassurance they need, then go ahead and provide it. An example may sound something like this:

    "Mrs. Jones I realize this is your first home. In fact, most of the people that have purchased here are first-time homebuyers. To provide you reassurance, I've asked several of my existing homebuyers if they would be willing to talk with new customers who also were feeling apprehensive. How does that sound to you?"

4. Request for pressure – from time to time, you'll meet customers who lack self-confidence to make their own decisions. They may directly or indirectly ask you to push them in the direction you want them to go.

    "It's such a hard decision; I just don't know what to do."

    "What do you think I should do?"

    The correct response, of course, is to gently push them to take action, if indeed you feel the sale is right for them.

5. Hidden Resistance – a hidden objection is concealed beneath the surface of another objection. When you encounter a large number of objections, particularly ones that don't fit together, you can conclude there is hidden resistance. Unless your diagnosis and presentation were completely wrong, you're customer probably wouldn't have that many issues.

    Whenever you encounter illogical questions, too many issues or a refusal to accept good answers, you may assume there is hidden resistance. And when you encounter a combination of two or three of these signs, you may be certain of it.

    Another signal of hidden resistance is the lack of funds to qualify. Your prospect wants to buy but they haven't saved enough money for a down payment. To keep from telling you they lack sufficient funds, they raise an objection that redirects the conversation and allows them to avoid telling you about their financial situation. If you suspect this is happening, the best thing to do is grab the bull by the horns and ask directly if money is the real issue. Once you get the real issue on the table, often you can provide a solution.

6. Easy resistance – an easy issue is one that's based on a misunderstanding or lack of information, perhaps even ignorance. Often this is a request for additional information, or it may be a test of your knowledge and experience. An example of easy resistance may sound like this:

> *"Mrs. Jones, earlier you mentioned about the test scores being low for our school system. I have the most recent test scores, and the good news is that scores in reading and math have improved dramatically. Would you like to see that report?"*

7. Hard resistance – a hard issue indicates a desire for a benefit your product does not offer. For example: a request for four bedrooms in a design that features only three bedrooms. Or it could involve emotions. Any time you deal with issues of personal safety or schools or crime, you can be confident you are dealing with hard resistance.

This drawback is the hardest to overcome. Ultimately, your customer is going to make the decision. Your job is to provide enough information for him to make an informed decision.

Start today to clarify and classify resistance. You'll be amazed at how much your customers will appreciate your willingness to fully understand what is holding them back from making a decision. I know I've said it many times throughout *Building Results,* but it bears repeating – when you align yourself with your customer, you both move forward.

Verify

Stephen Covey's book *7 Habits of Highly Effective People* provides readers with seven great habits by which they may live. The fifth habit is 'seek first to understand to be understood'. The *Handling Resistance* process requires you to follow a similar strategy by repeating back what you hear, thus demonstrating understanding.

Verifying is an important step in the process. Too often we filter what we hear through our own experiences and assume things that aren't even in the customer's mind. You've either added to the objection or altered it to fit your own thinking. Tell the customer, *"Okay, here's what I hear you saying."*

Your customer can listen to their words as you have interpreted, thereby offering an opportunity to change or clarify your understanding. Verifying requires that you summarize not repeat back word for word. You don't want the customer to think you are mimicking. Demonstrate understanding by modulating your tone, pace and physiology to match your customer.

Remember that most prospects buy on emotion and justify with fact. The four primary motivations for purchasing are convenience, family, investment and prestige. Verifying requires that you listen very carefully for evidence of these emotions. If you hear a misunderstanding or drawback that includes one of these emotions, verify it to demonstrate understanding. You've demonstrated respect and thus earned the right to move the *Handling Resistance* process to the next step.

Reframe

When new customers visit your model home they bring their own life experiences and those experiences frame how they think. To handle resistance, you have to reframe those experiences. Let's look at an illustration of reframing:

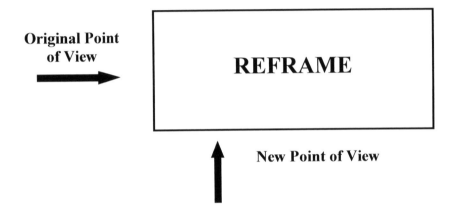

Reframing provides your customer with a new point of view – a different way to think about or look at a misunderstanding or drawback. Until your customers consider alternative views, you're facing a losing battle. When they begin to look at their objection from a different perspective, they're changing the way they think and understand. And that's the purpose behind reframing. Your goal is to provide your customer with a new point of view.

A key role in new home selling is to provide your customer with solutions. One way to reframe your own thinking is to begin seeing yourself as a solution provider rather than a salesperson. Think about that for a moment. When new home prospects visit your model home, they bring needs, wants and problems. In order to sell more homes than your competition, you must be able to provide solutions to those issues. The more solutions you provide, the more likely you are to close the sale. Reframing provides multiple solutions for solving the customers' misunderstandings and drawbacks.

There are five ways to reframe a customer's thinking:

1. Minimize

2. Convert to a positive

3. Third-party testimonial

4. Documentation

5. Pro and con

The following examines each reframe with clarifying examples.

Minimize

You can minimize an objection by reducing or diluting it to something positive, such as the higher price of your home versus a lower-price competitor. To do this, simply agree that your price is higher, but explain that actual monthly out-of-pocket expense will be fractional compared to the total price difference. Your minimize reframe might sound something like this:

> *"Yes, it is true Mrs. Jones; our Hartford model is $5,000*
> *more expensive than our competitor's Wellington model.*
> *However, when you consider the current interest rate,*
> *you'll pay only an additional $30 a month or $1 a day.*
> *Mrs. Jones, isn't the Hartford model with its dream kitchen*
> *worth the additional $1 a day?"*

By minimizing the additional cost down to $1 a day, you provided your customer a different point of view. Yes, the home still costs an additional $5,000, but in your customer's mind you provided a different perspective. You are asking her to consider the advantages of your model while acknowledging a minimal cost difference

You can use the minimize reframe to dilute additional miles to and from work, interest rate differences, cost of options or to reduce size of one homesite versus another. The minimize reframe will work whenever a comparison is present.

Convert to a Positive

For every negative there's a positive. Your role is to find the positives in every home, homesite, community, location, financing, builder misunderstanding or drawback. To do that you first must reframe how you see those various misunderstandings and drawbacks. Consider only the facts of each, and eliminate any emotional influences. Many times it's your thinking that needs reframing because you haven't counterbalanced the positive with the negative.

I know this is not easy to do, but it is important. In Chapter 3 you learned – you are always communicating. Never forget your customers are watching your physiology, listening carefully to your voice tones, and paying close attention to the words you choose. To reframe a customer's thinking by converting to a positive, your message must be congruent with your verbal and non-verbal behavior.

To make my point, I want you to consider an experience I had with a salesperson who attended one of my *Building Results* seminars in Indianapolis. I was teaching how to *Handle Resistance*. It is my practice during my seminars to demonstrate all the selling skills I teach. I asked the group if they had an objection with which they needed help. A student raised his hand and said he had a very difficult objection and was sure it could not be handled. He told about his customers who had to drive past a working junk yard to enter his community. He was right – that was a difficult objection. I wondered why a builder would purchase land that had a junk yard at the entrance. I immediately looked at my builder client for help but he just smiled at me.

Well, always ready to practice what I teach, I asked the salesperson the following clarifying question, *"How long has your company been selling in this community?"* He answered, *"Three years"*. His answer surprised me. I followed that question with another, *"How many sales have occurred in those three years?"* His surprising answer was, *"150 sales"*.

That meant the community was selling 50 new homes a year. By most measurements 50 sales a year is a successful community. I then asked, *"How long have you been selling in the community?"* He responded, *"Three months."* I asked, *"How many sales have you achieved?"* He answered, *"Three."* He was selling one house per month compared to the other salespeople averaging four per month.

It was clear to me – and hopefully is to you – that the homebuyers in this community had no problem with the junkyard. The person who had the problem was the salesperson. It was not the customer who needed to see the community from a different point of view; it was the salesperson. This is exactly what I meant earlier when I said that many times it's a salesperson's thinking that needs reframing, because he or she hasn't counterbalanced the positive with the negative.

Through further questions I learned that the community was tree lined with winding streets and featured a small pond surrounded by a park the builder built in the center of the community. And because the homebuyers had to pass by a junk yard, the builder was able to purchase the community for a sizeable discount allowing thousands of dollars of savings to pass through to the homebuyers.

Therefore, because of reduced pricing, homebuyers were happy to look past the junk yard and see the real value the community represented. Unfortunately, the salesperson could only see the junk yard, and his sales presentation matched his feelings.

Step back from your community and take an honest look at how you communicate with your customers. Are you part of the problem or are you part of the solution? When you change the way you see, you will change the way you sell. Open your eyes and look for ways to convert your community's negatives into positives.

Converting to a positive reframe might sound like this:

> *"Yes, it is true Mrs. Jones, this homesite does back up to high-tension lines. However, here's something to think about: first, the distance between you and your neighbor to the rear is 300 feet, the length of a football field. You said earlier that privacy is important to you, right?*
>
> *Second, I have an additional $5,000 in free options to use at my discretion. Select this homesite and I'll discount the price of your options by $5,000 – a monthly savings of $40 per month. I understand your concern, but when you consider all the positives, don't you agree this homesite represents an excellent choice?"*

The key to using this reframe is recognizing that for every negative there is a positive. When you look for the positive, you reframe your perspective and thereby earn the right to reframe your customer's perspective.

Always look for the good in everything; you'll certainly make more sales and earn more money.

Third-Party Testimonial

This is an excellent way to communicate the advantages of your homes, home sites, community, location and builder. Just ask your buyers to write down the reasons they purchased from you. Remember that people buy on emotion and justify with fact. Get your buyers to put those purchasing facts in writing.

Third-party testimonials work because new buyers want to be assured of their purchase. When they read how another person decided to buy, they feel confident they are making the right decision. An old cliché, 'birds of a feather flock together' is especially true when it comes to buying a new house. People look to others for needed assurance.

A third-party-testimonial reframe might sound like this:

> *"Yes, it's true Mrs. Jones; Wellington Farms is a brand-new community and you'll have to live through all the construction noise. However, you aren't Wellington Farms' first sale. In fact, we've sold ten homes to date. Because I knew many of my customers would share your concern, I asked several of them to write a testimonial letter describing why they decided to buy now versus waiting until construction had declined. Would you like to read what your new neighbors had to say about their purchase?"*

The main benefit of testimonial letters is to provide comfort and assurance to conservative home buyers; but it won't work unless you secure letters from your buyers. Don't be afraid to ask. People want to help you succeed because when you sell, the value of their home increases.

Zig Ziglar writes – help people get what they want and they will help you get what you want. One sure way of helping your customers get what they want is letting them know how, through third-party testimonials, other buyers in your community made their decision. Start today and begin securing testimonials. The result will be increased sales and income.

Documentation

Sometimes your customers have inaccurate or incomplete information that leads to misunderstandings. Incomplete information may come from their friends, relatives, acquaintances and sometimes, unfortunately, from well-intentioned Realtors. To your customers, these are reliable sources. Initially they place more trust in these outside contacts than they do you. The documentation reframe eliminates misunderstandings because the information comes from third-party sources not connected to you or your prospect.

There are many sources of information: schools, local and county government, the local home builders' association, newspaper articles, the Home Owners Association, worship centers, internet, library, etc. The important thing is to be informed about your community. When you hear or read news about the area, file it for future reference. Start a scrapbook today and post everything about your community. Leave it on your desk for prospects to review. This action may eliminate an objection before it ever surfaces.

The documentation reframe may sound something like this:

> *"Yes, it's true, Mrs. Jones, Hart Estates is adjacent to Kennedy Ave., but the proposed widening was rejected by the City Council last week. I attended the hearing because I knew that widening might negatively affect my community. Here's a copy of the meeting minutes documenting the council ruling. Would you like a copy to review?"*

This is a sure-fire way to earn your customer's trust while demonstrating your professionalism. Keep your eyes and ears open; documentation is all around you.

Pro and Con

The pro and con reframe is similar to the Ben Franklin close. You simply list the positives and negatives. The best way to understand the pro and con reframe is to draw a line down the middle of a sheet of paper, draw a horizontal line across the top and then place two headings at the top. Here's an example of a pro and con reframe:

New Home	**Used Home**
• Ability to personalize home	• What you see is what you get
• Included warranty	• Limited warranty, if any
• Service department	• Higher closing costs
• Below-market interest rates	• Market interest rates
• No or minor maintenance	• Immediate maintenance
• Energy efficient	• Higher energy bills

The pro and con reframe is useful when there are opposing points of view. It requires your customer to consider the negative without you being viewed as negative or biased. Your role is to remain positive and informative at the same time. Using a pro and con reframe might sound like this:

> *"Yes, its true Mrs. Jones, there are four used homes sold to every one new home. However, have you considered the advantages of buying a new home versus purchasing a used home? For other customers considering a used home, I've highlighted the positives of new construction versus disadvantages of a used home. Would you like to see this comparison?"*

Please note that when comparing new and used homes I purposely use the word 'used home'. I know many of you use the word pre-owned, pre-existing and pre-loved. Remember there is great power in the words you choose. Those words create visualize images in your customer's mind. The word 'used' creates a powerful image. Take advantage of that image by referring to used homes as exactly that 'used'. The benefit to the pro and con reframe is that you allow your customers to examine both.

Final Thoughts about Reframing

Reframing requires lots of practice and preparation. Step back and really examine your community. Look for the things that your prospects may find objectionable. Then determine what reframe might work best with the objection. Keep in mind that more than one reframe might be required to handle your customer's resistance. Write out exactly what you're going to say and then practice the reframe with another sales person or your sales manager. This effort pays big dividends when customers state misunderstandings or drawbacks. You'll not only sell more homes but also earn the respect of your customers.

Tie Down

The tie-down requires your customer to respond to your reframe. The response you hear informs you whether your customer accepted or declined your reframe. Without an agreement you may not have satisfied the customer's misunderstanding or drawback. You may have more work to do. The time to determine acceptance is immediately following your response. Following every reframe to an objection it's important to tie-down the customer's acceptance.

To gain agreements simply ask:

>*"Does that make sense to you?"*

>*"How does that sound?"*

>*"Do you agree?"*

>*"Okay?"*

>*"Does my explanation make you feel better?"*

If you don't get a positive response, relax, take a deep breath and mentally consider your next reframe. Remember there are five possible reframes. What you may have discovered is that you are dealing with hard resistance – a serious drawback.

At this point, begin anew presenting the *Handling Resistance* process starting with clarifying and classifying. Ask questions to better understand the objection. When you're confident you have enough information, proceed with the next reframe. Be sure to ask your tie-down question to confirm acceptance.

If your customer continues to object and you're confident you understand the objection, it may be time to accept the fact that you may never satisfy this customer. A sign of a true professional is the ability to recognize what is important to the customer and accepting that you did your best. You haven't failed; sometimes your solutions simply do not meet your customers' requirements. Remain positive and prepare yourself for your next opportunity.

Putting It All Together

Here's an example of how to put all the steps of handling resistance together:

Salesperson: *"Mrs. Jones, you have selected a home and homesite, you like the community and location, we've arranged financing, and you told me that you have confidence in XYZ Homes. Let's go back to my office and write up the agreement to start construction on your new home."* (Salesperson is summarizing customer decisions.)

Customer: *"Not so fast, Matt. You and I also discussed that I'm considering one of your competitors. To be truthful, I am leaning toward the other builder, but I haven't made up my mind."*

Salesperson: *"Yes, Mrs. Jones, I know you're considering a home in   Sycamore Creek. Would you share with me why you're leaning in that direction?"* (Salesperson is clarifying and classifying.)

Customer: *"Matt, it's a matter of price. If I buy before the end of the month, I can save $5,000. If you lower your price to match your competitor, I'll sign a contract today."*

Salesperson: *"What you say, Mrs. Jones is true; the homes in Sycamore Creek are priced lower than mine."* (Salesperson is agreeing with the truth.)

                 "Is a lower price your only concern, Mrs. Jones?" (Salesperson continues to clarify and classify.)

Customer: *"Well, I'm also concerned about the Home Owners Association fees. As you know, Matt, Sycamore Creek doesn't have an HOA."*

Salesperson: *"Yes, it is true, my community is fortunate to have an HOA, and I'm aware that Sycamore Creek does not."* (Salesperson is agreeing with the truth.)

                 "Of the two concerns you have which is more important to you, Mrs. Jones?" (Salesperson continues to clarify and classify.)

Customer: *"I'm more concerned about the price. I realize there's a value in the HOA. I believe I can live with*

*the added expense. Matt, if you lower the price, I'll
sign a contract with XYZ Homes today."*

Salesperson: *"Mrs. Jones, first I want to verify my understanding
of your concerns. You're concerned about the price
of the home and the HOA dues. However, you
realize there is value in an HOA, right?"*
(Salesperson is verifying.)

Customer: *"Yes, those are my concerns and I do agree there is value in
an HOA."*

Salesperson: *"I'm not authorized to discount our homes. I
understand you've arranged financing through
Gemini Mortgage. If I remember correctly, your
rate is 6% for 30 years. That   means you'll pay an
extra $30.00 a month if you buy from XYZ Homes
– or $1 a day."* (Salesperson using a minimize
reframe.)

*"Mrs. Jones, when you consider the quality,
features and personal services that come with every
XYZ Home, do you agree that it's worth $1 a day?
Doesn't it make sense to buy from XYZ Homes?"*
(Salesperson is using tie-down.)

Customer: *"Matt, you make a strong argument, but I'm
watching my pennies – every dollar counts."*

Salesperson: *"Mrs. Jones, what you say does make sense. Buying
a new home is a big decision, and you're right to
watch your pennies." (*Salesperson is agreeing in
principle.)

*"Mrs. Jones, let's go back to my office. I asked
several of my homeowners, who also considered
Sycamore Creek to write a letter detailing why they*

chose Wellington Estates over Sycamore Creek.
Would like to read why your new neighbors are
moving to Wellington Estates?" Salesperson is
using third-party testimonial)

Customer: *"Matt, that sounds like a good idea. I'm still*
concerned about the $5,000, but I would like to
know why those people chose Wellington over
Sycamore Creek. I want to make a good decision,
and you're right – it is only $1 a day."

Handling Resistance Process

Purchasing a home is a big decision. For most people it will be the largest investment they will ever make. It's only natural to be cautious and suspicious. Therefore, accept the fact that your customers are going to resist purchasing until they're convinced it's the right thing to do. Your job is to prepare yourself by anticipating any objection they may have about your homes, homesites, community, location, financing, and even your builder. The six-step *Handling Resistance* process prepares you for each and every objection.

Your big challenge is to take the time and consider what objections your customers may have. Write out how you will respond, and then role-play so you're ready to answer those objections when they come. I know some of you who are reading *Building Results* will not accept the challenge. Unfortunately, that will be a mistake. By learning how to *Handle Resistance,* you're providing the information your customers need to justify their decision. So accept the challenge, think about all the objections you may encounter, prepare for them and then reap the benefits of additional sales and income. What follows summarizes the *Handling Resistance* process:

A.   Homebuyer resistance generally falls into two categories: misunderstandings and drawbacks.

B.   Misunderstanding is usually the result of a customer lacking information or being misinformed about a particular feature or benefit.

C.   Drawback usually results from your product failing to provide a benefit the customer considers important or the customer simply not liking something about your homes.

D.   Resistance may take the form of one of four possibilities: mere comment, request for more information, buying signal or a real problem.

E.   The six step *Handling Resistance* process:

1. Agree – acknowledge what you heard. You can simply say *"Okay"* or *"I understand"* or you can agree that what you heard is true, may be true or makes sense in general. The purpose is to align with the customer, to see the objection from your customer's perspective.

2. Pause – allow the customer time to mentally process that you are agreeing, not defending or arguing. After all, the objection is what it is and many times cannot be changed.

3. Question – ask questions to understand if you are dealing with a misunderstanding or drawback. Don't assume you know what the objection is. 'Peel the onion' back by asking clarifying questions, and then classify the objection so that your response provides the justification for your prospect to move forward.

4. Verify – always summarize your prospect's answers to your questions. This demonstrates understanding and understanding leads to alignment and cooperation.

5. Reframe – once you understand the objection, be prepared to offer your prospects a different point of view. You can minimize, convert to a positive, document, use third party testimonials or offer pro and con reframes. Make your choice based upon the information you learned by asking clarifying questions.

6. Tie down – confirm that your customer accepted or declined your reframe. Without confirmation you are simply guessing; with confirmation you can move forward confidently.

F.   Ask for the order – you've earned the right.

Final Thoughts about Handling Resistance

Always remember that your customers are filled with questions about the things that interest them. So the point is not to avoid or fear questions and resistance, but to welcome both. When you answer their misunderstandings or drawbacks, they feel confident they are making the correct decision when they say, "*Yes*".

One other thing to keep in mind – people buy on emotion but justify with facts. When you provide your customers with a new perspective, they can justify their decision to family, friends and Realtors. Now you not only have a happy customer but you also have earned potential referrals. Learn how to *Handle Resistance* and you can look forward to additional sales and income.

Good luck and good selling!

Chapter 10

Closing

If you don't ask for the order, chances are you won't make the sale. That is the essential truth of the new home selling profession; because when you ask for an order you provide the motivation your customer needs to take action.

It is true in new home selling that closing is the name of the game. The following general statements best summarize the fundamentals of closing – the rules of the game:

1. Lead people to minor decisions.

2. Understand how people buy.

3. Assume success.

4. Close constantly.

5. Create urgency.

6. Maintain control.

The rest of this chapter examines each statement and provides you with closing strategies to help you earn the right to ask for the order.

Lead People to Minor Decisions

Successful closing is fundamentally an extension of other steps in the selling process. You must be proficient in all phases of new home selling if you hope to close consistently. Therefore, your first move toward sharpening your closing skills is to improve all your selling skills, especially your ability to discover and qualify. The more proficient you are in this critical area, the more successful you will be in closing.

The more your customer says yes, the harder it will be to say no. Get your customers to agree that your homes, homesites, community, location, financing and builder satisfy what is important to them. Ask affirmative questions or tie-downs throughout your sales presentation and especially during discovery. A tie-down question is any question that asks for an agreement. Use tie-down phrases such as these:

Don't you agree?	Wouldn't it?	Isn't it?
Right?	Doesn't it?	Don't you?
Aren't they?	Can't you?	Isn't that right?
Don't you think?	Aren't you?	Okay?

This is an easy way to lead customers into minor decisions, isn't it? You can gently influence them to nod their head in agreement, can't you? The result is a series of yes responses that will lead to a closing, don't you agree?

Set Up the Close through Agreement

Before a prospect will purchase a home you must secure a yes response in each of the six decision-making categories: home, homesite, community, location, financing and builder.

In Chapter 5 you learned that many of these decisions, such as location, community and builder, may have been made before a customer meets you. It's crucial for the prospect to agree that your location, community and builder meet or exceed his decision-making conditions. The only way to know is to ask for agreement on all six areas. Through discovery and qualifying you reach agreement one minor decision at a time. As you learned, the result is a series of yes responses leading to a close.

Turn resistance into a close. Uncover your customer's points of resistance and then ask:

"Is that the only thing standing in your way of buying this home today?"

If the answer is yes, overcome the resistance and close. As stated earlier, closing is an extension of the whole sales process. When you use the *Handling Resistance* process you learned in Chapter 9, you earn the right to ask the closing question. Don't you agree?

Use Trial Closes to Lead to the Close

Throughout the sales presentation, test your customer's mindset by asking trial close questions. A trial close question is any question that requires the prospect to make a conditional commitment. Some examples follow:

> *"If you were to make a decision today, do you think you would prefer the white or oak cabinets?"*

> *"I have shown you several homesites today. Do you prefer the one on Kennedy Lane or Whiterbone Court?"*

> *"When you make the decision to purchase, will your front elevation be stone or brick?"*

If your customer answers any of these questions, you are moving toward a partial close. Your customer hasn't bought the house but she has purchased a color for the cabinets, selected a particular homesite or decided on elevation. Each response by itself represents a partial decision, and when all the minor decisions are combined, you've earned the right to ask for the order.

To demonstrate the powers of a trial close consider this experience I had with a builder who sells age-restricted housing in Las Vegas. My role was to shadow the builder's salespeople throughout a sales presentation and then offer coaching suggestions on how they might improve. Prior to each presentation, I would sit with each salesperson and offer ways to improve individual effectiveness. On this occasion my coaching tip focused on using trial closes to gain conditional commitments.

When the time came to meet with the prospect, the salesperson had quite a surprise. He had not one prospect but four! Four ladies had stopped after lunch at the model center to look at homes, making it quite clear they were 'just looking'. The salesperson said he understood and led the ladies to the first model. He introduced the ladies to the home and asked his first trial close question. He said, *"How does this home compare with what you have in mind?"* The lady in charge smiled and said, *"We're just looking today. Can we look at some other models?"* He smiled and led the ladies to the next model.

He once again trail closed and once again was told they were just looking – not buying. He proceeded to the third house and once more asked another trial close question. He said, *"I have shown you three homes. If you were to buy today – and I know you're not – which home would you buy today?"* The lady who seemed to be in charge smiled and said, *"I'm not buying today, but if I where I like the second model you showed us."* With that a lady standing behind me said, *"I like this house."*

Her response surprised the salesperson. Quickly realizing that it was possible all four ladies might be prospects, he asked, *"Are you all interested in purchasing a new home?"* The answer surprised him even more. Not only where these four ladies interested but their entire card club – eighteen people – where looking at new housing because the 99-year lease on their current homes was about to increase dramatically. Each was on a fixed income and could not afford an increase. The salesperson had stumbled onto a possible gold mine. Later the salesperson and I discussed the situation. He agreed that it was his consistent asking for conditional commitments that uncovered the real buying motivation.

Remember that closing is a process – one step at a time. A tie down or a trial close confirms each step along the path to gaining the final agreement.

Understand How People Buy

A thorough knowledge of the home buying process is an indispensable selling tool. Keep in mind that when homebuyers start looking, they have the whole marketplace from which to choose. They haven't committed to a particular community or home. To help them make such a commitment, you must learn where they are in the buying process and focus their attention on one or two homes within your community to the exclusion of all others they might consider which might meet their requirements.

Understand that prospects will not buy until the advantages of one home overshadow the advantages of all other alternatives.

Achieve maximum involvement during your very first meeting. Stress your builder's competitive advantages. When you fail to stress the merits of your builder, home, homesites, community, location and financing right from the beginning, you leave the door open to competitors. Most homebuyers look at numerous communities and homes before making their final decision, therefore, you must participate fully in their selection process from the first meeting to be sure they make a return visit.

For most people, a home represents the largest single investment of their lifetime. The ultimate decision regarding whether or not to buy is made by balancing all the benefits against the disadvantages. To achieve a closing, your benefits must outweigh the disadvantages. The buyer must have complete confidence that owning your home has more benefits than any other available home.

Don't forget your customers always have many alternatives open to them, not the least of which is staying where they are. They can buy a competing homebuilder, buy a used home or wait until they've seen more homes in both categories. They can rent a home or apartment for an interim period. And they can remodel their present home.

Of these alternatives, your biggest competition may come from their current home. Again, unless the advantages of your home clearly surpass all these options, most likely you will not be able to close.

Remember people buy on emotion and justify with fact, rather than the other way around. Draw out your customer's feelings and help them talk about the subtle but important aspects of living that might influence a decision to buy from you. The *Discovery and Qualifying* process discussed in Chapter 5 sets up the close. The more precise you are at uncovering your customer's needs, wants and issues, the more likely you are to understand his true buying motivations. Strong discovery questions that help you understand people's motivations are based on what is important to them about the new home, the homesite, the community, the location, the financing and the builder.

A sure way to get to a closed sale is to make the decision-making discovery questions from Chapter 5 a consistent part of every sales presentation. To refresh your memory, review those questions:

"What is important about the new home we will build for you?"

"What is important about the homesite you select for your new home?"

"What is important about the community you select for your new home?"

"What is important about the location you select for your new home?"

"What is important about the financing you select for your new home?"

"What is important about the builder you select for your new home?"

Make these decision-making discovery questions a consistent part of your sales presentation and you will succeed. The late Dave Stone advised: *"Discovery is the Siamese twin to closing. If you don't understand what is important to your prospect, you will not close"*. Dave was right, when you use discovery questions, you quickly learn the how and why prospects buy.

Also, remember that most homebuyers will compromise on their specifications but seldom on their motivations. Listen for their buying motivations. In Chapter 6 you learned that customers have four primary buying motivations: convenience, family, investment and prestige. When you understand which of these four motivations are dominant, you're able to demonstrate how your home, community or location will satisfy that motivation. By focusing on buying motivations you make it easy for your customer to say, *"Yes"*.

Assume Success

Personal confidence is one of the most important keys to successful closing. When you assume the sale has been made, it makes the buying decision seem smaller and less painful. The bigger a decision, the more anxious and indecisive your prospects become. But when you communicate this assumption, prospects feel they are not making a new decision, they're just going along with a decision already made.

This assumption also makes another force work for you. Most people adjust to other people's expectations. If you communicate that you do not expect them to buy, chances are they won't. For example, would you buy from someone who asked? *"You wouldn't want to buy anything today, would you?"*

However, when your entire demeanor communicates that you expect a sale, you often will get it. Your confidence increases your prospect's confidence. The buying decision seems like a natural step in the direction you both are heading.

Master Your Own Fears First

Inspire confidence by controlling your own doubts and indecisiveness. You know you should close more often, but each time you close you risk rejection and failure. Some salespeople are so fearful of rejection and failure they don't ask for the order, even when they see that prospects want to buy. They ignore obvious buying signals because they are afraid that prospects will say *"No."*

Unfortunately, not closing will not solve your problem. It may avoid pain now, but causes much greater long-term rejection and failure. You may even lose your job, and that's a crushing rejection as well as a real failure.

The moral is: Don't be afraid to fail. A 'no' answer is not a personal failure; it's a professional challenge to continue selling. Keep in mind that your customer is not rejecting you; he is rejecting the solution you are providing. Your role as a new home sale professional is to provide your prospects with multiple solutions that satisfy their needs and wants. The more solutions you provide the more likely you are to close. When you begin to see yourself as a solution provider and not a salesperson, the closer you become to earning the right to ask for the sale.

Assume the Sale

The best closing strategies are always based on the assumptive approach. Assuming the sale is more an attitude, a state of mind, than a specific strategy. When you 'assume the close' you exude confidence as you move steadily toward the closing question.

In Chapter 2 you learned that 'you are always communicating'. Make sure that your physiology, tonality and your words send the message that you expect the prospect to buy today. If your customers see, hear or feel any doubt, verbally or non-verbally, they will begin to move away from you. Communicate that you assume the sale and you and your prospect will move toward the close. Always proceed with the continuing confidence that your prospects are going to buy today.

Radiate Enthusiasm

Enthusiasm and confidence are contagious. Think success. Think positively. Think enthusiastically. When you assume the sale, you act and talk as though the purchase were a foregone conclusion.

However, the only way to think success is to have a thorough working knowledge of all preparation areas covered in Chapter 3. If you are not knowledgeable about your homes, homesites, community, location, financing and builder, you will have a difficult time thinking and acting with confidence and enthusiasm. Knowledge gives you the confidence to radiate enthusiasm. Without knowledge you are leaving success to chance. Knowledge is the key that unlocks enthusiasm.

The following statements communicate different assumptions. Which ones do you think communicate confidence?

1. *"If you buy this home, I think you will be happy."*

2. *"Maybe you should wait until tomorrow; my manager says interest rates might be lower."*

3. *"I feel sure a monthly payment of $1,000 is the right payment for you."*

4. *"You do agree that the homesite on Kennedy Lane is perfect for you, right?"*

5. *"When you own this home it will be dreams come true."*

6. *"Don't you think buying a home is a good idea?"*

Statements 3, 4 and 5 communicate confidence. They indicate that you assume the sale has been made. And what makes this possible are the words you choose. Select words that match your assumption that your customer is going to buy today.

Many times it's as simple as changing one word that makes the difference. By changing the word 'think' to 'know' in statement 1 you communicate confidence to the prospect that the right decision is being made. Your customers want you to 'know' they are going to be happy they don't want you to 'think' they will be happy.

Words communicate confidence – choose your words carefully and you earn the right to ask for the order. Consider including the following words into every sales presentation. These words communicate confidence, enthusiasm, and action.

Now	Today	Solution	Decision
If	When	Time	Important
Yet	Buy	You	Thank You

Close Constantly

If you do not close early and often, you run the risk of losing your customer's respect. Customers know why you are there; they expect you to close, they even expect you to close many times. If you do not close repeatedly, they will see you as weak and unprofessional.

When you close again and again, they will respect your drive and tenacity – even if they don't buy. They may complain that you are pushing them too hard, but remember – if you don't push, you won't close.

Of course, you may feel that pushing for action is inconsistent with the *Building Results* approach to selling. You have learned to slow down, avoid pushing and how to relate to prospects on their terms. Why then should you push now? Because you don't help your prospects unless they buy. The best house in the world is worthless if it's never built. If you have performed well the earlier selling steps discussed in this book, you know that your prospects need your product. Be prepared to give them that little push they need to overcome their fear of acting. And don't hesitate to do it often.

Because the concept of pushing for the sale is so important. I want to share a funny experience I had with several salespeople in Phoenix. While helping a group of salespeople role play the skill of *Handling Resistance*, I was overcoming an objection when the salesperson stopped me and said, *"I'm feeling pressured and I don't respond well to that type of selling"*.

I quickly regrouped, smiled and said, *"Maggie, you and Ted have been to the model home three times. During your visits you've agreed that you like the Wellington model, the homesite on Kennedy Lane is perfect for you and you think that our community and location meet all your expectations. You said, the financing plan we discussed works well for you and you've told me several times you're satisfied with us as your builder. Maggie, is that true?"* She looked me in the eyes and said, *"Yes, what you are saying is true."* I then smiled and softly said, *"Then, Maggie is it okay if I apply a little pressure now."* She matched my smile and to my delight said, *"Yes"*.

My reason for telling you about this experience is because you must first earn the right to apply pressure. The only way to earn that right is to get your prospects to agree that your homes, homesites, community, location, financing and builder meet or exceed your prospects' buying conditions. When you gather all those agreements you have earned the right to push for the sale – and shame on you if you don't.

Ask the Closing Question Directly

To close any sale, you must 'ask for the order'. It's surprising how many salespeople fail to comfortably take this final step. The right to close is earned by all the preceding steps, but this doesn't guarantee the prospect will say, "*We'll take it*!" Therefore, you must effectively close.

Keep in mind that a closing question is one which, when answered affirmatively, automatically gives you the right to start writing the contract. Closing questions can be asked on one or more of the following topics:

1.   Legal names that are to appear on the contract.

2.   Preferred date of occupancy.

3.   Size of the down payment or initial investment.

4.   Type of financing.

5.   Size of the earnest money deposit.

Typical closing questions:

"How would you prefer your names to appear on the contract?"

"How soon would you like to take possession of your new home?"

"The minimum initial investment for the Wellington is 3%. Would you prefer the minimum, or would you rather increase the size of your down payment?"

"Based on our discussion, it seems that a mortgage of $150,000 would meet your needs. That will work for you, right?"

"The earnest money deposit is 5% of the sales price. How much of that can you comfortably handle today to bind the sale now?"

It's obvious that an affirmative answer to any of these questions permits you to begin writing the sales agreement. This is the key moment in the home buying process. If you hesitate now you may lose your closing momentum. You may assume the sale once an approval or non-resistant answer is given, so start writing. Congratulations, you just sold a home!

Trial Close Early and Often

Trial closes are attempts to gain commitments or identify resistance. When you ask your customers to buy, they can only do two things: buy or express an objection. Buying obviously solves your problem, and an objection may show you how to earn the sale.

Trial closes are requests for conditional commitments. For example, if your prospect has expressed an objection to a specific home, homesite, time of delivery or certain contract terms and you know you can solve the concern without deviating from your builder's policy, you might reply:

"If I can make that change for you, will you sign a contract today?"

That question forces the discussion on the important issues. If prospects were not really concerned about the issue, they now must state another one. If they were only holding back because of this one objection, you may get an agreement now. It's easier for prospects to agree to a conditional commitment than it is to say, *"I'll take it!"* Trial closes not only help identify and satisfy issues, they cause momentum leading to the sale.

Trial closes also are good progress checkers. They help gauge your effectiveness and insure that you don't oversell. Here are a few trial close questions that measure your customer's thinking:

"How does this sound so far folks?"

"In your opinion, how does this home compare to what you've seen already?"

"What are your feelings about the value you get with this home?"

"Is this what you've been looking for?"

"Can you think of any reason not to invest in a new home now?"

"With inflation creeping up, it doesn't make sense to wait, does it?"

"Are you convinced now, or should I show you some more homesites?"

"Would you like to bring your whole family over to look at the home you've selected?"

"A high quality home is a good investment, isn't it?"

"What's your thinking now, based on what we've been discussing?"

Trial closes offer a low-pressure way to close constantly without appearing to be excessively pushy or hard sell. Yet they set the stage very effectively for the final close.

Close on a Minor Point

You can soften your prospect's closing decision by avoiding the 'major closing question' in favor of a 'minor closing question'. As emphasized earlier, most people resist making big decisions, and the bigger the decision, the more strongly people avoid making them. By assuming that your prospect has decided to buy, and all that's left is to finalize some minor point, you avoid a direct confrontation with 'the scary big decision' and at the same time let buyers feel they are making their own decision.

A good way to get a positive answer is to make the closing question a choice of two minor alternatives. No matter which is selected, the sale is confirmed. The best way to begin such a question is *"Which would you prefer?"* Examples:

"Which would you prefer in your new kitchen, oak or walnut cabinets?"

"Which exterior elevation do you prefer, the contemporary or traditional?"

"Would you prefer a single door to the patio, or the French doors shown in the model?"

"Would you prefer spending an additional $2,500 for a finished garage or finish it yourself after you move in?"

Closing on a minor point is very similar to the trial close. The only difference is that you are not asking for a partial or conditional commitment – you're simply asking your prospect to make a choice between two alternatives. Once she chooses, you've earned the right to ask a more direct closing question. The minor point close is an effective means of helping your buyers over the last hurdle to the total commitment.

Vary Your Close

There are probably as many closes as there are salespeople. One popular sales manual written many years ago by Dick Russell lists 160 separate sample closes. Here are just a few to consider:

The direct close has the advantage of clarity and simplicity. You simply ask for the order.

> *"Mr. and Mrs. Smith, let's go back to my office and sign the purchase agreement. Is that okay with you?"*

The forced choice close converts a big decision into a smaller one. Instead of having to decide whether to buy or not, your prospect is asked to choose between two different products or two variations of the same product.

> *"Would you prefer two stories or the single story?"*

The limited choice close reduces confusion and indecision when a prospect is considering several alternatives. You make the choice and then ask for the order indirectly with a forced choice or any other type of close. For example, if prospects cannot choose between several options, recommend the one they seem to like best and then ask for the order.

> *"Mr. and Mrs. Smith you seem to be leaning toward the stone elevation. As I said earlier, I do have one other family considering that same elevation. I can only build one more stone elevation on Mill Creek Road. To secure the stone elevation, let's go back to my office now and write the contract."*

The limited supply close is useful for procrastinators. Say that you're not sure you can meet your prospect's needs later. It is now or never.

> *"Mr. Smith, there are only two lots left in phase 2. Which one do you want?"*

The balance sheet close is especially appropriate for those who respond to the logical approach. Put the reasons for buying on one side and the reasons for not buying on the other. A balance sheet for a renter might be:

Reasons for Buying	Reasons for Not Buying
1. Income tax benefits	1. Want to think about it more
2. Earn equity	2. Initial investment
3. More space	3. Easier to stay
4. Convenient location	4. Moving expenses
5. Appreciation of value	5. Lease problems

The reasons for buying are stated in terms of the alternative the prospect is currently using (such as: renting an apartment, considering one builder over another, etc.), and there is a heavy emphasis on the major advantages (value, space, convenience, quality, and price). Balance sheets also can compare the reasons for buying now with the reasons to delay a decision. Of course, after discussing any balance sheet you must ask for the order.

> *"Mr. and Mrs. Smith, I know you can now see the advantages of buying versus not buying. Let's go back to my office get the paperwork started."*

The summary close summarizes all the agreements you and your prospect have reached through the *Discovery and Qualifying* process. Before someone will buy a home they must agree on location, builder, home, homesite, community and financing. Once you have a 'yes' in each area ask for the order.

> *"Mr. and Mrs. Smith, you both agree that the Wellington is perfect for you and the kids. We know you like the homesite you selected on Pointview Avenue. This location is convenient to work and the community has the jogging trails you both want. The financing you selected provides you with a comfortable payment; and based on what you said earlier, you're satisfied with us as your builder. Let's go back to the office and write up the contract."*

Most likely the reason salespeople fear closing is they know they haven't earned the right to close. They haven't reached all the necessary agreements. Remember the words of Dave Stone: *"Closing is the Siamese twin to discovery and qualifying."* Dave was right, the more skillfully you discover and qualify, the more prepared you are to summarize agreements and naturally proceed to a close.

The point in reviewing these six closes is that if one type of close doesn't work, try another. Varying your close increases your chances of appealing to your prospects' real buying motivations while overcoming any resistance to buying now.

If you use the same close over and over again, prospects may feel you are pushing too hard. But when you master a variety of closes, you can select the best ones for each situation and close again and again without appearing repetitious or overbearing.

Create Urgency

In the closing process, you have to generate a sense of urgency to buy, to buy today, otherwise your customers will tend to 'want to think it over', to delay their decisions until absolutely necessary. Therefore, how you handle the various aspects of urgency can be very important to your sales performance and income.

Urgency is a function of time and personal motivations. What may seem urgent to one prospect may not to another. Some people, for example, will place little value on money, while others will jump to close if they learn that a price increase is imminent. Not everyone will react the same way to the things you may say to stimulate urgency, so it's good to develop a range of 'urgent messages' and there are at least eight you might consider.

One of a Kind

In Chapter 8 you learned that with homesites there is really only one of a kind, because land, views and amenities vary with each homesite. Every homesite has its own inherent values based on its exact location and its orientation to other elements in the surrounding environment. This simple fact helps us create a desire to own a particular homesite and emphasize the need to make a decision now; for fear that someone else will appreciate its value and decide to buy it first. If others are looking at the same property, the tempo of decision-making can easily be accelerated.

> *"Mr. Benton, I don't want to pressure you, but I do have one other couple interested in the homesite on Norman Avenue for the same reason you are, sun orientation. Both of you want to build swimming pools and want a north and south orientation. This is the last homesite that satisfies that criteria. I strongly advise you to buy now."*

Price Increases

In new home selling, we always have the reality of increasing costs that ultimately must be passed on to homebuyers. By using your knowledge of pending or anticipated price increases, you can encourage hesitant prospects to buy now. If they wait, they'll have to pay more.

Price increases also represent an opportunity for your prospect. If they buy before the increase, they earn instant equity. Always remind your customers that housing remains a great investment and the longer they wait to buy, the less equity they earn. Urge your prospects to buy now and receive the benefit of price increases.

> *"Mr. Benton, I know you saw the flyer announcing another price increase. If you wait, you'll pay more. Let's go back to my office now and sign the contract so you can take advantage of the lower pricing today. The benefit is that by buying now you earn instant equity. I know you agree that makes buying now a good thing."*

Financing

During the past few years, fluctuations in financing availability, rates and closing costs have affected your homebuyers. Because of media attention, they instantly are aware of variations in interest rates. You can use this awareness to create the urgency to buy now. If your prospect waits, he runs the risk of less favorable borrowing conditions. You might have the calculations prepared ahead of time and show him how much more he'll pay over a 15- or 30-year contract if he ends up paying just 1/2 or 1% more.

> *"Mr. Benton, mortgage money is available now, and if you decide to buy today, I can assure you of financing at the rate of 6%. But if you wait, these favorable terms may not be available at all."*

Construction Schedule

Most homebuilding companies work on a controlled program for construction scheduling. Therefore, you can easily justify the importance of selecting and confirming a home now, so it will be started in time to meet the buyer's occupancy requirements. The convenience of moving at an optimum time also helps stimulate an immediate decision.

> *"Mr. Benton, you mentioned earlier that you wanted to be in your new home before school begins. The current building schedule is 96 days from start of construction. It is possible to shave a few days off that schedule, but I can't guarantee it. To meet your goal, you need to make a decision today."*

Processing Details

Many steps are required to secure the necessary permits to build a new home. If approval for a mortgage is a factor, and it usually is, then the normal procedure is further complicated with paperwork required by lenders and government agencies. By stressing the length of time required to follow through on all administrative details, you can create a valid and compelling reason for deciding now.

> *"Mr. Benton, building a new home is a series of processes. Most of these processes my builder controls. However, because of the popularity of this community, it's taking an extra two weeks to secure building permits. I know you want to be in your new home before the holidays; therefore, to meet your goal you must buy now."*

The Season of the Year

Based on the attitude of your buyer, the nature of your climate and its subsequent building problems, you can normally create some sense of urgency for any season of the year. Perhaps your prospect should order early so that his home is available when he wants it for the enjoyment of the remaining seasons, or so he can avoid possible labor disputes or a shortage of materials or weather-related work stoppages.

> *"Mr. Benton, I am sure you understand that the rainy season is quickly approaching. Normally, the rain slows our building time down by 2 to 3 weeks. In order to complete your home before the holidays you need to make a decision today."*

Solving Any Contingency

If customers have another home which they must sell before they can buy a new one, you can point out the urgency of getting the old house on the market, particularly if it's a good time of the year to sell the home.

> *"Mr. and Mrs. Benton, the local real estate market is very active right now. Reports I receive from the real estate board bear this out. Naturally, the time to sell your present home is when the market is good, and if you start right now, you can take advantage of the best selling season of the year."*

It's often wise to have actual records of real estate activity to show hesitant buyers who have homes to sell. Such third-party visual documentation not only increases your credibility, but also adds to the sense of urgency you want to create.

The Living Pleasure

The personal benefits of enjoying home ownership may, in the final analysis, be the most important force in motivating your customers to act now, rather than wait. People don't like to postpone pleasure, and you can capitalize on this universal desire. Real estate specialists across the nation have identified a strong trend in the home buying market in the aftermath of 9/11. "Buyers don't want to put off any important, life-influencing decision," one researcher says. "They feel a sense of urgency and the feeling of not knowing what tomorrow may bring."

> *"If you select a home now, you and your family will be in your new home in plenty of time to enjoy the summer season in our community. Your children will have the parks, pools and tot lots, and you'll be able to participate in the kinds of leisure activities you like so much."*

And this same motivation can be modified for any season of the year:

> *"Be in your new home before Christmas and enjoy the holidays in a brand-new home. Can you think of a nicer Christmas present?"*

> *"Be in your new home before spring so you can plant your own flowers and vegetables and enjoy them all summer long."*

> *"Move in before school starts so you and your children will be all settled before the new school year begins."*

If you maintain a tempo of excitement and urgency about acting now – if you are working to promote an environment of success – your sales will be certain to increase. People respond positively to successful operations. They want to share in the success. So remember that emotions are contagious – always make sure your emotions are worth catching.

Maintain Control

To close effectively, you must have control. Ultimately, your conversion of closed sales to the opportunities available will depend on how effectively you control your sales environment. The more you learn the art of controlling your sales environment, the easier it will be for you to help your prospects make favorable buying decisions.

Choose a Controlled Setting for Closing the Sale

The best location is your own sales office or a quiet corner where you can proceed without interruption. Be physically close to your customers, preferably seated, so you can see and judge their reactions. In Chapter 2 you learned that 'you are always communicating'. That communication principle also is true for your prospects. When you position yourself where you can gauge their emotions you can determine their willingness to buy now. You want to see their expressions, both positive and negative, and if necessary be prepared to use the six-step *Handling Resistance* process learned in Chapter 9 to overcome resistance during the closing.

Make Your Prospect Comfortable

Be sure there are enough chairs. Try to create a pleasant, relaxed and friendly environment. Decor, for example, is quite important, as are room temperature and lighting. Have activities available for children. Buy coloring books, crayons, toys and games to occupy them so your prospects can give you their undivided attention.

Beware of the Messy-Desk Syndrome

A cluttered office is always an obstacle for a salesperson. When buyers are supposed to be making a positive decision, you don't want them reading yesterday's paper or notes about another transaction. You don't want anything around to distract them from the main objective – purchasing a new home now.

Turn Off Your Office and Cell Phone

Make sure you are able to receive messages, but don't let the ringing of a phone break your closing momentum. Closing is all about timing, and the time to turn off your phones is during closing. Your primary goal is the complete control of your sales environment. You must create a closing climate or you risk losing your buyer's attention.

Whenever you seem to be losing control of the closing process, get your prospect involved again in visual displays or by talking about their interests. When outside influences interrupt the flow of conversation, pause for a moment, relax your buyers, and then regain control by reviewing and summarizing the last few points upon which you agreed.

Constant awareness of your customer's reactions and sensitivity to their inner feelings will help you do the things that relieve emotional pressure. Your own responsiveness will also be your best safeguard against losing control in the critical moments leading to the close.

The Closing Process

Closing is the name of the game – if you don't close you lose the game. In this chapter you learned a closing process that will work well with each new home prospect you meet. The following summarizes the important closing steps covered in this chapter. Begin today to make each of these steps a consistent part of your sales presentation. You'll be rewarded with satisfied homebuyers, a happy builder and additional sales and income.

A.   Learn the fundamentals of closing – the rules of the game.

    1. Lead to minor decisions.

    2. Understand how people buy.

    3. Assume success.

    4. Close constantly.

    5. Create urgency.

    6. Maintain control.

B.   The more your customer says *"Yes"*, the harder it will be to say *"No"*. Persuade customers to agree that your homes satisfy their needs and what is important to them. Ask affirmative questions or tie-downs throughout your sales presentation and especially during discovery.

C.   Achieve maximum involvement during your first meeting. Stress your builder's competitive advantages. When you fail to stress the merits of your builder, home, homesites, community, location and financing right from the beginning, you leave the door open to other competitors who will stress those merits.

D.   Remember people buy on emotion and justify with fact, rather than vice versa. Draw out your customers' feelings and help them talk about the subtle but important aspects of living that influence their decision to buy a home from you.

E.   Ask the closing question early and often; if you don't you run the risk of losing your customer's respect. Customers know why you are there; they expect you to close, they even expect you to close many times.

F.   You have to generate a sense of urgency to buy – to buy today – otherwise your buyer will tend to want to think it over, to delay their decisions until absolutely necessary.

G.   To close effectively, you must have control.

Further Thoughts about Closing

Let's face it; you won't always close on a single visit no matter how skilled and persuasive you are. However, your goal should be to obtain at least a partial close.

Whenever you sense that you cannot carry your prospect to the close on a single visit, you should do the next best thing; extract some type of decision that begins the process of involvement. This partial close can be just an appointment to return for another inspection. It might also be a phone meeting or a 24-hour lot hold reservation.

The lot hold reservation is undoubtedly one of the most popular means of reaching a partial buying decision. Pinning a name on a homesite can make a prospect feel as if he has really purchased a new home. The mental commitment is actually more important than the written sales document. People will cancel sales they don't believe should have been made, but if they mentally picture the sale, chances of canceling diminish dramatically.

If you cannot get a lot hold, ask for the next appointment. Please keep in mind that the sales process most likely will last from four to six hours. During that time your buyer has to make many decisions. Be prepared to meet with your prospect many times over a period that may last from ten to fourteen days. Selling a house is much like eating an elephant; you do it a bite at a time.

Lastly, if you are not able to get an appointment, then your objective must be to set up a phone call. Most first time visits average twenty to thirty minutes. When you consider all the decisions a buyer must make, it's easy to understand why you must develop solid reasons to call someone again. Your call must be welcomed if you are going to proceed to the next step, an appointment.

If you're successful in any one of the following categories you should consider each a close: sales agreement, lot-hold reservation, a second appointment or even permission to place a follow-through phone call.

Finally, keep in mind that all the close can do is convert desire to action. It cannot create desire – that comes earlier in your sales presentation. Concentrate on getting your customer to act.

Don't summarize the sales presentation over and over again or discuss your selling points in endless detail. More than likely that will bore prospects and it certainly shifts the focus away from action.

Do not raise new issues; they just confuse your prospects and provide excuses for procrastinating. The more you talk, the less chance you have of getting action now. You do not want prospects to listen to you – you want them to buy today. So help them to buy, then relax and let them do it!

A Few Final Words

This chapter has listed a number of closing ideas and questions. It's unrealistic to expect to use them all on a single customer, so it's up to you to select the selling strategies and questions that work best for you. Some strategies will be more effective than others, depending on the conditions that prevail and the varying characteristics of the prospects you're trying to close.

However, if you keep the six fundamentals of closing in mind – and practice various ways of applying them to your individual sales situations – chances are excellent that your percentage of successful closes will improve dramatically.

Good luck and good selling!

Chapter 11

Follow Through

Several years ago I received a phone call from one of my builder clients requesting assistance with identifying a sales problem he was experiencing. One of his better communities was being outsold five to one by a competing builder. I was familiar with the builder and the location of the community, so the difference in sales surprised me. We met and decided I would mystery shop the competing builder to learn first-hand how and why my client was being outsold.

I arrived at the community around 10:30 the next morning and was met by a professionally-dressed sales trainee. She introduced herself, explained she was new to the company and would assist me for a short time while the sales counselor completed a customer phone call. The young trainee asked me several good qualifying and discovery questions. She directed me to the community map and familiarized me with the neighborhoods many features and benefits.

We were joined by the sales counselor who introduced herself and asked the trainee to summarize what she had learned so far. The sales counselor then began an informative presentation on the builder, location and the resent sales successes they were experiencing. To put it mildly, I was impressed with both the sales trainee and sales counselor.

The sales counselor then asked me a series of discovery questions to determine my housing needs and wants. I explained that I was in the process of relocating and downsizing since my grown children had flown the nest. She responded that the homes she was offering probably were too big but she had another community that would meet my needs perfectly. She suggested we look at the model home to experience the builder's quality, features and custom upgrades, escorting me through the two-story model, stopping in each room to point out features and benefits.

I felt her sales presentation was well planned and very professional. When we completed the tour she suggested I inspect the second model on my own. She had to make a quick phone call and asked me to stop by her office to pick up directions to the other community.

After touring the second model, I came back to the sales center. She was talking with another couple and after a few minutes excused herself to speak with me. Not surprised that I thought the house was too big, she provided me with directions to the community she felt would satisfy my specific needs. She asked if I would call the next day to tell her what I thought. She also offered to fax me additional information, if necessary.

From what I've told you, I'm sure you believe she did an outstanding job. You would be partially right but, unfortunately, you also would be wrong. Yes, she greeted well, asked excellent discovery and qualifying questions, demonstrated the home, built value in the community and location, and sent me to look at homes that met my specific buying condition.

However, she made a serious mistake by not securing my name and phone number so she could follow through on the excellent sales presentation she conducted. She asked me to call her back when all she had to do was say *"Let me get your name and phone number and I'll call you tomorrow to answer any questions you have. And, if necessary, fax you any additional information you may need to make a smart home buying decision."*

How many times has this happened to you? I'm sure if you're like most new home salespeople, it happens far too frequently. You make a great sales presentation and then you fail to follow through. One thing you can count on in new home sales is that few prospects buy on the first visit.

According to research studies on the attitudes and actions of new home buyers:

1. They typically inspect at least six to ten new communities or other alternatives before deciding upon a purchase.

2. They typically narrow their interest to three or four homes, new and used. A good way to identify these homes is to call it the 'short list'. These are the homes and builders about which they are serious. Clearly an objective is to make your prospects 'short list'. Once they focus on four or fewer, they're ready for closing.

3. They typically return two to four times to each home under consideration before making a purchase, unless they've had an unusual amount of product exposure or time constricted, as in a relocation move.

4. They typically spend four to six hours with a salesperson before the sales agreement is finalized.

It's no wonder the vast majority of sales you make will be to buyers who are not completely sold during their first visit. Thus you must develop a sales presentation that motivates them to return. And that's where following through makes a big difference between a sale and no sale.

The follow through, contrary to what the name may seem to imply, is not limited to what you do after you say, *"Goodbye"*. More properly, it could be described as what you do after you say, *"Hello"* and detect that your customer wants to say, *"Goodbye"*. In short, the follow through involves taking the necessary steps from the outset of the sales presentation to bring the customer back, ready to listen, understand and buy.

Most new home experts agree there are four steps to an effective follow through. Each step is dependent upon the successful completion of the step before it. In essence, you need to:

1. Think about your follow through.

2. Justify your follow through.

3. Implement your follow through.

4. Follow up your follow through.

Now we'll examine in detail how the effective follow through can help you turn serious prospects into happy new homeowners.

Think about Your Follow Through

'Minnesota Fats,' the renowned pool hustler, advised: *"If you're going to win at this game, you hit the one and think the two."* What's true in the pool hall is equally true in the sales office. A sure-fire way to increase sales is to think in terms of setting up your follow through during your initial sales presentation. This means during your prospect's first visit, you must watch for telltale signs that they aren't quite ready to buy. Once you receive these signals, it's time to start thinking about your follow through.

Watch and Listen for Verbal Cues

Nowhere is listening with your eyes and ears more important than in your follow through. If the customer appears to be tired or unable to make a decision, or if he continues to be evasive or preoccupied, it's probably time to shift gears and set the stage for a second meeting.

Before you move on, test your judgment by asking a trial close question. Here's a question that will let you know what your prospect is thinking. As you will see it may be necessary to justify the reason you're asking.

Salesperson: *"Is this something you are considering doing now?"*

Customer: *"Maybe; we're not quite sure. It's been a long day."*

Salesperson: *"The reason I ask is because you sound and look tired. I know you
                 have visited several communities today. Would you like to set
                 another appointment when you have more time?"*

If that fails to elicit a positive response, it's very likely time to think about your follow through.

Watch For Non-Verbal Cues

How many times have your heard someone say, *"Your actions speak louder than your words?"* That's why non-verbal cues play such an important part in setting up a second appointment.

In Chapter 4 you learned about detecting minimal cues through body language. The way a person sits, stands, moves and gestures usually precedes spoken language. So, knowing how to interpret minimal cues can save you and your customer a lot of time, trouble and frustration.

Sharpen Your Listening Skills

Listening with your eyes as well as your ears is a skill. And like any other skill, it can be sharpened. But it takes conditioning, concentration and practice. To sharpen your listening skills, you might want to consider the following suggestions.

When a customer stops talking, pause and wait to see if your prospect is finished talking. Silence is golden. When two people are talking at the same time, no one is listening. The result is not conversation; it's noise. As a contrast to your customer, show that you are listening by occasionally resorting to silence. When a customer stops talking, don't jump right in with your response. Pause and ponder. This can be productive for you and impressive to your customer.

Think ahead. When a person talks to you, they usually are trying to make a point. The good listener tries to guess what these points are before they are made, with mental questions such as *"What is this person trying to get at?"* *"What is it they want me to understand?"*

If you correctly guess what your prospect's point will be, your understanding and retention of the point will be strengthened when it finally is made. If you guess incorrectly, you can start comparing the point you guessed with the actual one made. This is a very profitable learning process – learning by comparison and contrast.

Tell the Customer You're Listening

No one likes to talk in a vacuum. It's frustrating and annoying. Tell the customer you're listening by offering non-verbal as well as verbal reinforcement. Lean forward and look interested. Support the customer with statements like, *"I agree," "I hear what you're saying,"* or *"I've thought the same thing myself."*

Look at your customers as they talk; good eye contact tells them you're listening and interested. Sometimes a direct stare may make a customer feel uncomfortable or threatened. If you sense this, you can occasionally look away pensively or take notes, after you've told the customer you'll be doing so.

One quick note on taking notes – its okay to take notes during a sales presentation. In fact, your customers will appreciate you are paying close attention to what they're saying. Make sure the notes are simple so that you don't miss any non-verbal cues that your customer may be communicating. Taking notes communicates and demonstrates that you care about understanding important points.

Review What You've Heard

As a customer moves from point to point, they usually allow time for you to move along with them. They may change the subject with a phrase like, *"Now, let me talk about this matter of..."* This gives you an opportunity to verify what has been said and can improve your comprehension and retention of the material heard.

Role Play With a Partner or Group

Video tape role-play sessions or tape record an actual sales presentation. Then sit down with another salesperson to compare and critique your listening skills. Watch for small cues, verbal and non-verbal, that tell you when your listener has stopped receiving your message. Observe how attentive you are at receiving your customer's message. Listening is a two-way street. With practice and awareness, you can improve your skills dramatically. When you become a better listener, you improve your understanding. As mentioned so often in this book, better understanding leads to additional sales and income.

With the overwhelming majority of your customers, there comes a time in your initial interview when it is obvious you're not going to close the sale. When that happens, don't become frustrated or discouraged. Simply decide upon a good reason for setting up a second visit and then justify your reason for following through.

Justify Your Follow Through

This second step in follow through lays the groundwork during the prospect's first visit that initiates a second visit. If handled properly, the justification not only will make another visit necessary, but also will make the second visit welcome.

Too many times, inexperienced salespeople merely secure a customer's name and telephone number and then follow through with a 'remember me' phone call. Calls like that, of course, are impersonal, unexpected, vague and probably unwanted.

It's far better to take an action during your initial interview that will provide you with a good reason for setting up a future appointment. Then your call will be wanted and well received.

The Partial Answer

When a customer asks a question for which there are several answers, it often is wise to withhold some information as a reason to make a future appointment. Occasionally you'll find you really do need more time to research or update your facts and figures. Often, additional time may not be absolutely necessary but could be helpful. And there are times when you could provide a detailed answer immediately, but you and your customer are better served by waiting until later.

You must, of course, maintain your credibility with the customer and not appear to be purposely withholding information.

The Unsolicited Promise

Occasionally your customer will fail to ask the kind of question that lends itself to the partial answer. Then it's up to you to create a need by making the unsolicited promise. For example, you may have read your customer's minimal cues and decided it's time to justify your follow through, but the customer has quit asking questions. That's when you need to suggest that more information is necessary, offer to track it down, and end your presentation by promising to get back in touch.

Whether you use the partial answer or the unsolicited promise, certain types of information are particularly suitable to follow through justifications. These include:

1. School enrollment information.

2. Availability of certain homesites.

3. Current administrative time.

4. Estimated dates of completion.

5. Possession dates.

6. Price of new homes.

7. Estimated dates of starting construction.

8. Availability of specific building materials.

9. Availability of optional changes.

10. Availability of certain types of financing.

11. Current lender qualifications for financing.

The key to the impartial answer or the unsolicited promise is speed. Immediately secure the information you promised and contact your prospect to report. Take too much time, and you risk losing credibility. Follow through quickly and you demonstrate professionalism. Never, ever forget that people want to do business with professionals. Use this opportunity with immediate follow through to differentiate yourself from all the other salespeople your customer is likely to meet.

Implement Your Follow Through

Once you've thought about and justified your follow through, the next important step is to implement your strategy. In short, follow through on the action you promised in your justification. That's where the telephone, mail or e-mail comes in handy. Let's examine the telephone first and learn how to make positive use of this important sales tool for follow through.

When you pick up the telephone, be prepared to follow through on your last conversation, building on the groundwork previously laid. Thus you can personalize your comments in a warm, friendly manner. If you've taken good notes during or following your initial sales presentation, this will be easy because your call will be structured to produce a specific result – persuading your customer to return for a second appointment. Such structuring requires thorough pre-planning and a polished telephone performance. The following strategies will help make that important first follow through phone call.

Informal Call

Your first call is made immediately after your customer leaves the model home. This call is designed to set you apart from the competition. Your goal with this call is to thank your customer for visiting the model home and put her on notice that you intend to follow through to determine her buying interest. The phone call is short and to the point. The following is an example:

> *"Hello, this is (your name) with (builder's name). I'm calling to thank you for visiting (builder name). I'll call you tomorrow evening to answer additional questions you may have and arrange for you to return for a second visit. Once again, thank you for visiting (builder name). Make it a great day."*

This phone call, most of the time, is left on voice mail. When she returns home, she will immediately be reminded of the visit to your model home and will anticipate your phone call the next evening.

What happens if your prospect only provides you with a mobile phone number? My advice is to always review your prospect's registration information before they leave the sales center. If only the cell number is listed, ask about a home phone number. Most people have a home and cell phone number. If not, go ahead and call the cell phone anyway. The worst thing that can happen is your prospect answers and you thank them once again for the visit. You still achieve your objective of differentiating yourself from the competition.

Formal Phone Call

Your second call is your formal phone call. This call is made between 24 and 48 hours following the first visit. Over the years I've asked salespeople how long they wait between a prospect's initial visit and the first phone call. I am constantly amazed because most salespeople wait as long as a week to make a follow through phone call. This is a drastic mistake.

There is a cliché that fits this situation perfectly – out of sight is out of mind. When your prospect leaves, she has the whole world from which to choose. The only way to separate yourself from all the other salespeople she's likely to meet is to immediately reconnect with the prospect. This simple act keeps you, your community and your builder in her mind. And as you learned in Chapter 6, buying decisions are always made in your customer's mind. The following outlines how to make this important second phone call.

Pre-Plan Your Calls

Before you pick up the phone, stop and ask yourself if you've done all your homework. Are you clear about your objectives? Do you know what you're going to say after *"Hello"*? Are you prepared to overcome foreseeable objections?

Careful planning is essential to effective phone follow through. For each call, set intermediate objectives based on the justification you used in your initial visit. Write down these objectives and keep them in front of you. Remember your primary objective is to bring your prospect back for a second appointment. Tell her just enough to heighten her interest but not so much that you answer all her questions.

A good way to gain and keep control of the telephone contact is to follow a well-planned, not canned, presentation. Here are the ingredients of a good phone presentation:

Identification – first identify the party you're calling and identify you.

> *"Donna, this is Joan Harris from XYZ Builders. I promised to get back to you, and I wanted to make sure I did."*

Qualify for convenience – make certain the customer is not too busy to talk and listen. No one likes feeling trapped, and everyone likes common courtesy.

> *"Do you have just a minute or two?"*

Disclose the benefit that will result from the second appointment – this will allow you to personalize the call and heighten your customer's interest.

> *"I think I've found a way to get you most of the options you want and save you some money."*

Justify the action – make sure your prospect understands the benefit to be gained.

> *"If you and Bob can set aside just one hour, I can explain what this will mean to you."*

Suggest a time and place – keep the initiative and keep control of the selling situation.

"How about meeting me here Wednesday night at the model home, say 7 p.m.?"

Confirm and hang-up – don't waste time with small talk. Once you have met your objectives of bringing your prospect back for a second visit, go ahead and bring the call to a close.

"Great, 7 p.m. Wednesday. I'm looking forward to seeing you both."

Whether you adopt this exact format is beside the point; the goal is to adopt some sort of planned presentation that allows you to gain and retain control of your follow through calls.

Polish Your Presentation

Visual communication is lost over the telephone. For better or worse, your personal appearance and body language are immaterial to someone on the phone. Since your success or failure depends almost entirely upon your oral delivery, you must develop and refine your verbal skills and listening habits.

Developing a pleasant telephone personality is possible only through hard work and practice. But a few basic guidelines will help.

Remember your voice reflects your personality – it's not just what you say, but how you say it that counts. Both you and your builder are judged by the voice on the telephone. So your voice should let people know that you are friendly, courteous, competent, helpful and trustworthy.

Be aware of your rate of speech – talking too fast may cause doubt and misunderstanding. Nobody trusts a fast-talking salesperson with a canned presentation. Talking too slow also is a problem. It permits daydreaming and makes you sound boring and unenthusiastic. So speak at an even, conversational rate, using your customer's name often enough to personalize your message.

Give your voice adequate variation – people like to talk to people, not to machines. Shift in pitch from high to low. Keep your voice well modulated, and avoid being a monotone. Tape record your voice and see what kind of image you get. If you don't like what you hear, work on improving it. With practice, speech patterns can be improved. In many cases, it's advisable to lower your voice. Sometimes nervous tension makes our voices get high and slightly shrill.

The telephone has two ends – use both. Good salespeople also are good listeners, something that requires concentration. Shut out outside distractions and inner worries. Empathize with your customer and listen without interrupting. Your prospect should be the only person in your world at that moment.

Let the customer know you're listening by occasionally interjecting comments like *"Yes"*, *"Okay"* or *"I see,"* you let the customer know you're paying attention. Listen carefully to the words your customer selects and listen to the tonality of those words. Both tell you what the customer is thinking. Are they convinced? Is it time to close? Are they confused? Do they need more information?

Remember, two of the most powerful words in the English language are I understand. To be successful in new home sales you must demonstrate understanding. There is just no way a prospect will understand you until you understand them. People buy from people they like and the best way to be liked is to demonstrate understanding. The follow through phone call provides that opportunity.

Take notes during the phone call. Chances are you're not a stenographer, so no one expects or wants you to write down everything the customer says. It's too easy to get lost in what you're writing and forget what you're hearing. However, it is a good idea to jot down key points for future reference. After the conversation, you can go back and fill in the blanks.

Leave phone messages – many people use Caller ID to screen their messages. This is another important reason to follow the advice given earlier in this chapter under *Justifying Your Follow Through.* You must do everything possible during your initial sales presentation to make your follow through phone call welcome. Even then, many times you will be forced to leave a voice-mail message. Go ahead and leave a well-planned, confident message. Like all things, success comes to those who plan and your voice mail message is no different. Consider leaving the following message:

> *"Good evening, this is (your name) with (builder's name). I'm following through on my promise to call you back and answer any questions you may have about our homes, homesites, community, location, financing or builder. I'm sorry I missed you. I'll call you tomorrow evening and, hopefully, be able to speak with you. If you want to contact me, my phone number is (sale center or cell number). I look forward to talking with you soon and satisfying your home buying needs. Make it a great evening!"*

By leaving this message you have accomplished the following:

1. Followed through on your promise to call within 24 or 48 hours.

2. Reminded your prospects they have six important decisions to make: home, homesite, community, location, financing and builder.

3. Provided them with the option to contact you at the sales center or cell phone.

4. Placed them on notice you will continue to follow through.

Questions that may be in your mind: How many phone calls do I make? Do I continue to make calls until I talk directly to the prospect? Or is there a time when I acknowledge that the customer doesn't want to talk with me or has made an alternative housing decision? The answer is to keep calling. I recommend making three attempts to reach the prospect, leaving voice mail messages each time, and then on the fourth phone call, leave the following message:

> *"Hi, this is (your name) with (builder's name). I've called several times and left voice mail messages each time. I haven't heard back from you, and it's my experience that either you are no longer interested or have found another home that better meets your housing needs. I'm calling to ask a favor. Please call my night number and leave a message letting me know about your current housing situation. My intent is not to harass you but rather to satisfy your housing needs. If you've bought elsewhere, congratulations! If you're still considering us, that's great! If you need more time to consider other homebuilders, I understand. Just let me know. I'll honor your decision and either continue to call or remove you from my follow through list. My night number is (sales center after hour's phone number). Thank you for considering (your builder). It is appreciated. Make it a great evening!"*

By leaving this message you have accomplished the following:

1. Followed through on your promise to continue to call.

2. Provided your customer with a safe, convenient and courteous way of letting you down if they've purchased elsewhere.

3. Demonstrated your professionalism by acknowledging the reality that people have other choices and that you accept their choice and are willing to move on.

4. Brought closure to a prospect you felt was interested in your product.

I know many of my peers will disagree with this strategy. My reason for giving this advice is that you must accept the fact that your product is not for everyone. When prospects choose another home, accept the fact and move on. If you've done everything possible to control what you can control, you must be able to let go of what you can't control. Someone once said, *"Sales are like buses. Miss one, wait a minute, and here comes another one."* As long as you've done everything you can, then let go and get ready for your next customer.

Remember, especially when it comes to setting up a second appointment – out of sight is out of mind. Don't allow more than 24 to 48 hours to pass without implementing a follow through phone call. Otherwise, you'll lose the impact of your first visit and the urgency of the initial interest. Too many salespeople make the mistake of waiting too long. If your customer is serious about purchasing a new home, your second phone call will be welcomed and anticipated.

Follow up Your Follow Through

Fundamentally, this means finding new reasons to contact your prospects. It means staying in touch. Successful salespeople never say die. Once they get a customer, they stay in regular contact until the customer either buys or makes another choice. Even months after the initial interview, they continue to mail or email out 'ticklers' just to stimulate renewed interest.

Provide New Information

New information of any kind gives you a legitimate reason for contacting past customers. For example, you may want to update a past customer with new information about:

1. New models

2. New financing plans

3. New homesites

4. Changes in pricing structure

5. Design changes in models

6. New products

7. Lower mortgage rates

8. Sales promotions

9. New communities

10. Finished inventory homes

Often, the best vehicle for passing along new information is a short, one-paragraph message, hand-written on an informal card. Here are examples to illustrate the many opportunities you have for rekindling the flames of customer interest with the possibility of opening the door for a future sale.

Inventory Homes

Just to remind you, I'm completely at your service at all times and have several new inventory homes for you to preview. I'll call you next week and check on your availability.

New Model Home

I would appreciate arranging a private showing on a new model home before it is advertised or publicly shown. I'll call you next week and check on your availability.

Interest Rate Change

If your schedule permits, I would appreciate discussing the current money market with you before interest rates move higher. I'll call you next week and check on your availability.

Price Increase

There is an expected change in our price structure. I'm sure it will be of interest to you. I'll call you next week and check on your availability.

New Homesites

I have some great news. (Your company) has just acquired some heavily wooded homesites. Several meet your criteria for purchasing. I'll call you next week and check on your availability.

Price Reduction

We are in the process of lowering the prices on some of our model homes. Certain price reductions are imminent. I'll call you next week and check on your availability to discuss this.

Homesite Availability

I've taken a home site off the market for you to inspect. It is superb. I'll call you next week and check on your availability.

New Homesites

I have an inventory of new lots which won't be placed on the market until next month. I think you should inspect these before they're picked over. I'll call you next week and check on your availability.

Added Incentives

Currently, my inventory of homes is at the highest level of the entire year. Shouldn't you take advantage of this opportunity and inspect this property? And the best part is we have lowered pricing and added incentives. I'll call you next week and check on your availability.

Company Changes

Would it be possible to meet with you during this coming week and discuss some new situations which have just developed at (your company)? I'll call you next week and check on your availability.

Product Changes

(Your company) is now considering removing some of our homes from our product line - up. There will be many extras included in these homes at no extra cost. I'll call you next week and check on your availability.

If you're on a first-name basis with your customer, the message can be signed on with the customer's first name and signed off with yours. Additionally, make sure that you're the one following through by announcing you will call and check on their availability. Too many salespeople make the mistake of asking the prospect to follow up the note with a phone call. This can be a big mistake. Always be proactive by saying you will initiate the action.

At the end of this chapter you'll find longer letters appropriate for communicating with your prospects.

Keep Sending Those Cards and Letters

Providing new information is a legitimate reason for staying in touch with former customers. But it's only one among many. Expressing appreciation and good will is an equally valid reason for sending a card or letter. Many salespeople have found that a short, hand-written thank you note within 24 hours of each personal contact makes an indelible impression upon customers. The advent of email makes sending a quick note easy, effective and efficient. You can also use the mail or e-mail to convey congratulations. Keep in contact by marking special events such as anniversaries and birthdays.

Everyone appreciates recognition – not only for themselves, but also for their families. A daughter marrying, a son entering college, or a spouse winning a tournament bring added pleasure when recognized by others. Scan local newspapers and keep your ears open for information about former customers who deserve a card or letter. Using mail or e-mail to make your name a household word is obviously an effective way to follow through.

Keep Accurate and Up-To-Date Customer Records

Nobody can remember everything. If you're like most people, you probably have a tough enough time remembering your customers' names, let alone which model they liked, the options they wanted, and the type of financing you discussed. That's why an accurate and up-to-date registration card is an absolute must.

On high traffic days, don't be tempted to jump from customer to customer without first recording your notes while they're still fresh in your mind. The more details you can summarize immediately on your customer cards, the more effective you'll be in following up. Identify the little things which will help initiate the next conversation. Names of children are as important as those of adults, if not more so. When you refer to the children by name, you win an amazing amount of good will from the parents.

Also note hobbies, likes and dislikes and clues as to what the decision-making conditions may be. You never know in advance which piece of information will help you most in following up. Get it down in writing immediately after or while your meeting occurs.

Organize and Utilize a Contact Management System

Frank Bettinger is widely acknowledged as one of the greatest salesmen of all time. In his best-selling book, *How I Raised Myself from Failure to Success*, Bettinger says the key to successful selling can be summed up in just one word – organization. All of the time and effort you put into keeping accurate and up-to-date customer cards means nothing if the information is not neatly organized and easily accessible.

That's why a well-kept contact management system plays an important role in a salesperson's life. This system is more than a convenient place to organize prospect information. It's a ready source of 'who, what, when, where and why' customer information you'll need to follow through. With the many software systems specializing in contact management, there are scores of ways to set up an efficient system. One way is likely to be as good as another as long as you can retrieve information with minimal effort. Begin investigating what contact management system will work best for you.

Card-reader software is another handy tool to quickly, accurately implement the information on all the business cards you collect.

The Follow-Through Process

Frequently, salespeople will ask me what separates the successful new home sales counselor from the average sales consultant. I always give the same answer, a professional sales presentation, a working knowledge of new home construction, and a consistent follow through program. They are equally important but it is the follow through program that really differentiates the successful salesperson from the average sales consultant.

You might be saying to yourself, *"Follow through really isn't that big a deal. I am making a good income now and I don't follow up."* You're right – you can make a good income without following through. But you are giving yourself way too much credit. Most likely, your builder has positioned your community with the right pricing, product and promotion, and you're taking advantage of being in the right place and at the right time.

If you want to continually sell more houses and make more money, start today to develop a follow through program separating you from all other new home salespeople. Take advantage of all the great marketing your builder does on your behalf by following through with each new home prospect that visits your community. Consider adopting the many concepts presented in this chapter. What follows is a summary of those great ideas.

A.   There are four steps to an effective and efficient *Follow Through* program:

      1.   Think about your follow through.

      2.   Justify your follow through.

      3.   Implement your follow through.

      4.   Follow up on your follow through.

B.   A sure way to increase your sales is to think in terms of setting up your follow through during your initial sales presentation. During your prospect's first visit, watch for telltale signs that they aren't quite ready to buy. Once you receive these signals, it's time to start thinking about your follow through.

1. Listen for verbal cues.

2. Watch for non-verbal cues.

3. Sharpen your listening skills.

4. Let your prospect know you are listening.

5. Repeat to verify.

6. Role play to improve.

C.   Follow through on the action you promised in your justification.

1. Provide partial answers to justify a follow through phone call.

2. Make an unsolicited promise to provide missing information.

3. Adopt a 'do it now' attitude by providing information within 24 hours.

D.   Once you've thought about and justified your follow through, the next important step is to implement your strategy. In short, follow through on the action you promised in your justification. That's where the telephone or email comes in handy.

1. Place an informal call immediately after your prospect leaves the model home.

2. Place a second formal call within 24 hours but no later than 48 hours.

3. Pre-plan your follow-through phone calls. Know your phone call objective and secure a second appointment.

4. Role play to improve your phone presentation.

5. Never forget out of sight is out of mind.

E. Continually search for new reasons to contact your prospects. Successful salespeople never say die.

1. Provide new information on anything new that is happening with your homes, homesites, community, location, financing, or builder.

2. Send or email your first follow-through note within 24 hours.

3. Keep accurate and up-to-date records on each new home prospect – no exceptions.

4. Locate and use a professional contact management system.

5. Just stay focused and follow through consistently. Day after day, week after week, and year after year. The result is a successful new home sales career.

Final Thoughts on Follow Through

Following through is a full-time job. Day in and day out, it requires the total application of thought, word and deed. You must constantly think about your follow through. You must continually justify your follow through. You must always, without fail, implement your follow through; and you must persistently follow up on your follow through.

Because very few sales are closed during the first visit, effective follow through can mean the difference between success and failure. It's critical to consciously apply the four steps of following through until setting up the second visit becomes second nature.

Good luck and good selling!

Sample Letter

Thank You – Visiting # 1

Date

First Name, Last Name
Address
City, State, Zip

Dear (Last name),

Thank you for visiting (builder name) at (community name). I hope you enjoyed your tour of our beautiful and exciting (model home name).

The quality and uncompromising value reflected in our homes has resulted in (builder name) being recognized as the 'best value' single-family homebuilder in (area).

I realize you've probably visited other model homes and communities. Keeping track of all the unique benefits of each is sometimes difficult, but crucial, as you get closer to deciding which model you wish to call 'home'.

I'll call you on (date) to answer questions, elaborate on the many benefits of owning a (builder name) and to schedule a return visit to (community name).

Once again, thank you for visiting (community name). I look forward to talking and visiting with you soon!

Sincerely,

Sales Counselor
(Builder name)

Sample Letter

Thank You – Visiting # 2

Date

First Name, Last Name
Address
City, State, Zip

Dear (Last name),

Thank you for visiting (builder name) in (community name). It was a pleasure meeting you and having the opportunity to show you our (model home name) plan. I hope you enjoyed your first look at our beautiful community, and I look forward to your next visit.

I'll call you on (date) to answer questions, elaborate on the many benefits of owning a (builder name) and ask you to schedule a return visit to (community name).

Sincerely,

Sales Counselor
(Builder name)

Sample Letter

Compare the Difference

Date

First Name, Last Name
Address
City, State, Zip

Dear (Last name),

Thanks for visiting (community name). I hope you had an opportunity to compare the homes you saw here at (community name) with those of other builders. Close inspection will show that there is no substitute for the quality, style and workmanship that is yours in a (builder name).

(Builder name) sets the standard. They are built by a company committed to integrity in people, products and service.

Convince yourself by taking another look at a (builder name) before making your final selection. You'll be glad you did.

I'll call you on (date) to answer questions, elaborate on the many benefits of home ownership and schedule an appointment for a return visit.

Sincerely,

Sales Counselor
(Builder name)

Sample Letter

Thank You - Second Visit

Date

First Name, Last Name
Address
City, State, Zip

Dear (Last name),

Thank you again for considering (builder name) as the builder of your new home. I realize that buying a new home is an important decision, and at (builder name) we take the responsibility of building it very seriously.

Homebuyers today are looking for not only an **established builder** but also **quality construction** and an **excellent warranty program**. At (builder name) we strive to excel in all three of these areas. For this reason, I am enclosing information about our company history, our quality construction and our warranty program.

I hope you will find this information helpful in your search for a new home.

I'll call you on (date) to answer questions and ask you to schedule a return visit to (community name).

Sincerely,

Sales Counselor
(Builder name)

Sample Letter

Call to Action

Date

First Name, Last Name
Address
City, State, Zip

Dear (Last name),

WHAT ARE YOU WAITING FOR?

Historically speaking **NOW** is still one of the best times to make a new home purchase decision. Prices and interest rates remain low. Many families are realizing the dream of owning a beautiful new home much sooner than they had expected. It also provides the opportunity to get more home for your money!

(Builder name) is dedicated to providing the best quality and value in your first, next or last new home.

SO WHAT ARE YOU WAITING FOR?

Take advantage of available attractive interest rates. I urge you to come back so I can provide more information and elaborate on the many exciting benefits of owning a (builder name) in (community name).

I'll call you on (date) to answer questions and ask you to schedule a return visit to (community name).

Sincerely,

Sales Counselor
(Builder name)

Sample Letter

Community Selling

Date

First Name, Last Name
Address
City, State, Zip

Dear (Last name),

At (builder name) we realize how important it is to consider not only the builder but also the community in which you will be living. In today's competitive market, as always, location and resale value are key factors in any home-buying decision.

(Builder name) understands that you want to be proud of your neighborhood when family and friends come to visit, that you want to live in an area where you feel safe raising your children and one in which you feel secure investing. And that is just the type of community that (builder name) has created.

I'm enclosing listings of homes that have recently sold in the community. I hope you find this information informative and helpful in your search for a new home.

I'll call you on (date) to answer questions, elaborate on the many benefits of owning a (builder name) and ask you to schedule a return visit to (community name).

Sincerely,

Sales Counselor
(Builder name)

Sample Letter

Return Visit

Date

First Name, Last Name
Address
City, State, Zip

Dear (Last name),

****NEWS FLASH****

HAVE YOU HEARD?

HAVE YOU BEEN WATCHING?

The quality and value reflected in our homes at (community name) have resulted in (builder name) being recognized as the value leader in (area).

Things are happening very quickly around here as we continue to assist more and more families find just the right home. If you dream of being one of the many families residing in (community name), please come back for a fresh look at all the advantages we have to offer. I want to help you find a way to turn your dream into reality!

I'll call you on (date) to encourage you to return to (community name), to answer questions and elaborate on the many benefits of owning a (builder name).

Sincerely,

Sales Counselor
(Builder name)

Sample Letter

Homesites Disappearing

Date

First Name, Last Name
Address
City, State, Zip

Dear (Last name),

Since we last spoke, homesites have been selling quickly! Future (builder name) homeowners have made their choices and we are starting to build their new homes. I know you'd like to be a homeowner in this outstanding community, and I look forward to helping you select a homesite and getting the homebuilding process started.

I'm enclosing a current price sheet and list of homes we currently have ready for immediate move-in to make sure you have our most recent community information.

I'll call you on (date) to discuss setting up a return visit to take advantage of our inventory homes or to select one of our one-of-a-kind homesites.

Sincerely,

Sales Counselor
(Builder name)

Sample Letter

Mini-Survey

Date

First Name, Last Name
Address
City, State, Zip

Dear First Name,

Time is flying! It's amazing how fast the present can slip into the past.

(Community name) has come a long way since your visit. It is really evolving into a beautiful and special neighborhood.

Whether or not you're still in the market for a new home, (builder name) would appreciate your participation in completing the attached mini-survey to help direct our efforts in assisting people find just the right home. (Builder name) truly listens to the cares and concerns of its homebuyers, and your cooperation is greatly appreciated.

Enclosed you will find a self-addressed stamped envelope for your convenience. Just take a moment, fill out the survey and drop it in the mail – or better yet bring it with you and come back for another look at our beautiful models at (community name).

Thank you for your time. I hope to hear from you or see you very soon!

I'll call you on (date) to answer questions concerning the survey and ask you to consider scheduling a return visit to (community name).

Sincerely,

Sales Counselor
(Builder name)

Sample Letter

Phone Call Follow Through

Date

First Name, Last Name
Address
City, State, Zip

Dear (Last name),

It certainly was great talking with you on the phone today. I've enclosed an information package giving you some exciting details about (community name).

If you're interested in quality, family living with an exceptionally convenient location, then (community) may be just the place for which you've searched.

Rather than simply reading or hearing about (community name), I'll call you soon to arrange a VIP tour so I can give you an exclusive showing of our special neighborhood.

I think once you experience (community name) you will agree that this is the opportunity that you've been searching for – I promise you won't be disappointed.

Sincerely,

Sales Counselor
(Builder name)

Sample Letter

Relocation

Date

First Name, Last Name
Address
City, State, Zip

Dear (Last name),

I hope that your visit to (community name) is still lingering favorably in your mind.

I'm enclosing an information packet, which will be helpful to you throughout your relocation process. I hope it is useful in giving you a condensed introduction to (city-area).

If there is anything I can assist you with regarding your relocation – anything at all – please give me a call. I'll be more than happy to answer all of your questions.

I wish you all the best on making the transition to your new home a happy and pleasant experience.

I'll call you on (date) to answer questions, elaborate on the many benefits of owning a (builder name) and asking you to consider a return visit to (community name).

Sincerely,

Sales Counselor
(Builder name)

Sample Letter

Sales Manager – Thank You

Date

First Name, Last Name
Address
City, State, Zip

Dear (Last name),

On behalf of the entire team here at (builder name), I'm writing to personally thank you for your recent interest in a (builder name).

We are one of (area's) most well-respected and well-run builders. We pride ourselves on three principles:

1. First is our total commitment to our homebuyers. We do everything in our power to make sure that our homeowners are happy.
2. Second is our commitment to choices. We have a variety of single family housing alternatives. This allows you to pick the lifestyle that best fits your needs.
3. Our last and most important principle assures you will deal with friendly, customer-oriented people. You can rest assured our commitment is to promise a lot and deliver more.

I sincerely hope that you enjoyed your visit, and if there is anything that (builder name) can do to help you, please do not hesitate to call.

I've enclosed a sample brochure highlighting our commitment to quality.

Sincerely,

Sales Manager
(Builder name)

Sample Letter

Save Money

Date

First Name, Last Name
Address
City, State, Zip

Dear (Last name),

I'm writing to let you know that there has been some very exciting news here at (community name) since you last visited.

Much has happened in terms of new construction, exciting new home designs and streetscapes – all adding to the value and livability of this outstanding community.

You can save thousands by making a decision to purchase now rather than waiting till next year. Don't hesitate; please call me today to set up an appointment. We'd love to welcome you into our growing family.

I'll be calling shortly to set up an appointment to review the special homesites still available.

Sincerely,

Sales Counselor
(Builder name)

Sample Letter

Special Promotion

Date

First Name, Last Name
Address
City, State, Zip

Dear (Last name),

What I have to say really only requires two words … **SAVE MONEY**.

But that, of course, requires a bit of explanation. The special offer I'm enclosing gives you a unique opportunity to live in a beautiful (builder name) at a saving of thousands of dollars.

Now that wouldn't be unusual if I were just offering our left-over homes at bargain prices, although considering the tremendous savings we offer, you'd still be getting an outstanding value. We're offering a package of upgrades to any qualified buyer who closes before (date).

In addition, we have a scheduled price increase going into effect (date) which will immediately increase the value of your new home and provide you with instant equity.

I urge you to take your pick now and revisit (community name) while these money-saving bargains are still in effect.   Remember, there may not be another chance to save like this because the special is only available until (date). So please act quickly.

I will be calling you soon to schedule an appointment and answer questions you may have.

Sincerely,

Sales Counselor
(Builder name)

Sample Letter

New Models

Date

First Name, Last Name
Address
City, State, Zip

Dear (Last name),

I'm so excited, I just had to write!

Knowing your great interest in (community name), I had to let you know about the new models we are opening soon. They're well designed and offer the type of family living I know you want.

I asked our division president for permission to preview them to a limited number of people, and I wanted you to be among the first to see them.

As demand will be very strong on these new homes, I recommend we get together shortly to preview them.

I'll call you on (date) to set up a VIP appointment time.

Sincerely,

Sales Counselor
(Builder name)

Sample Letter

Take another Look

Date

First Name, Last Name
Address
City, State, Zip

Dear (Last name),

Thanks for visiting (community name). I hope you had an opportunity to compare the homes you saw here at (community name) with those of other builders. Close inspection will show that there is no substitute for the quality, style and workmanship that is yours in a (builder name).

(Builder name) sets the standard. They are built by a company committed to integrity in people, products and service.

Convince yourself by taking another look at a (builder name) before making your final selection. You'll be glad you did.

I'll call you on (date) to answer questions, elaborate on the many benefits of home ownership and schedule an appointment for a return visit.

Sincerely,

Sales Counselor
(Builder name)

Chapter 12

Success Guarantee

First impressions are lasting impressions. This is true whether you are meeting one person or a group of people at the same time. I understand the importance of making a good first impression. That's why I open every sales training seminar with a *Success Guarantee*.

Is there a better way to make a good first impression than to offer a *Success Guarantee*? Think about it for just a moment – if someone you had never met offered you a *Success Guarantee,* how would you react? Would you stop and listen or would you discount the person and begin to move away from him? My bet is that at the very least, you would be curious and want to know more. After all, everyone wants success but not everyone knows how to achieve success. So by offering a *Success Guarantee,* I immediately capture my audience's attention. They want to hear and know more.

Achieving success is what this final chapter is all about. Have I got your attention yet? Do you want to know more, or are you somewhat skeptical? I know I would be curious and skeptical, asking myself how anyone could possibly offer a *Success Guarantee*. I know from experience that achieving success is a personal thing. And I also know that no one can guarantee success. My success, if it is to be, is up to me.

If I'm describing your thoughts, rest assured I agree with you. I cannot guarantee success but I can show you how to develop your own personal *Success Guarantee*. Would that be of interest to you? If you've read this far I'm pretty sure the answer is yes.

The ideas in *Success Guarantee* will change your life. Never forget they are just words now; it will be the actions you take that guarantee your success.

The Success Guarantee

Be willing to do what others are not willing to do. How simple it sounds, but it's so difficult to do. Understand that I am asking you to do things others are not willing to do. I'm asking you to separate yourself from everyone with whom you work and compete. You may be thinking, there are good reasons I don't want to do this or that, and your reasons may be legitimate. But if you truly want to achieve success, you must find it within yourself to begin doing that which others are not willing to do.

Building Results is bursting with ideas. Have you put any of those ideas into practice yet? Or are you waiting for just the right time? Consider the following experience I had with a group of salespeople in Chicago. It illustrates my point perfectly.

I was retained to conduct a series of *Building Results* seminars spread over several months. I met with the group one day each week. One seminar, *Following Through,* explained the idea of how making a phone call to the prospect immediately after he leaves the model home differentiates the salesperson from the competition.

I received nods of approval from the group. However, I still had no way of knowing whether the idea would be acted upon. Following through with ideas is entirely up to the individual. Each person makes his or her own choice.

The following week, before the seminar began, a sales representative pulled me aside and told me about the success she was having with the 'immediate phone call' idea. She had put the idea into practice with every prospect who visited her community, and she was amazed at the positive results. Her sales had immediately improved. She said some of her prospects had actually returned her call thanking her for thanking them. I asked for permission to share her success with the group.

Following the break I told the group about her success with the 'immediate phone call' concept. I asked her to provide third-party testimonial, which she did with great enthusiasm. I then asked the group by a show of hands how many had put the 'immediate phone call' idea into practice. I'm sorry to say not one other person raised a hand. There were thirty salespeople in the group, and only one had put the idea into practice.

What can you learn from this story? Do you now understand the significance of following the *Success Guarantee* concept? Do you understand that the concept *sounds* like a good idea but is not for everyone? Not everyone is willing to make the choice to separate themselves from the people with whom they work and compete. It's easier to show up at work every day and hope something good happens. It's hard work to do things that others are not willing to do.

How do you see yourself? Are you willing to go the extra step? Are you willing to put into practice the ideas in *Building Results*? Or are you going to be the person who puts the book on the shelf to gather dust. I hope you take the ideas contained in *Building Results* and make them part of you.

A great thing about sharing ideas is that once an idea is shared and used by another person, the idea now belongs to both the originator and the user. I want you to take these thoroughly vetted ideas, use them, and then share them with another person.

The result? Everyone wins, and in the end that's what life is all about – everyone winning!

Another experience I want to share involves my wife and the example she sets for our family and the people with whom she interacts every single day.

Donna went to work ten years ago when I decided to leave Ryland Homes and open up a homebuilding consulting company. Before that, she was a stay-at-home mom specializing in raising four children and managing our household. She decided to go to work in order to provide health insurance for our family. With a new business I needed all the financial help I could get.

She went to work part time for a Cincinnati department store, clerking throughout the store while keeping an eye open for a position that would hold her interest. Within two weeks she accepted a sales position for a well-known cosmetic company. It wasn't long before her excellent work ethic resulted in her being asked to take a full-time position. Within a year she was promoted to counter manager and soon after promoted again to account coordinator.

A decade later, she is now the event coordinator for Dallas, managing a staff of fifty part-time sales associates. She achieved her success because of her willingness to do what others are not willing to do. I could share a thousand stories demonstrating this willingness, but I'm going to focus on just one. I tell this story in most of my seminars because it's a perfect example of what happens when you go the extra mile.

Donna was working behind the counter when she received a phone call from a customer who had recently been helped by either Donna or another sales associate. The lady introduced herself and told my wife she had been in that day, made several purchases, and had left behind a bag of purchases from other stores. Her reason for calling was to check if any shopping bags had been found.

Donna asked her to wait on the phone while she checked. Unfortunately, nothing had been turned in. The lady thanked my wife and started to hang-up. Donna asked what other stores she visited and volunteered to retrace her footsteps and see if she could locate the missing purchases. The lady thanked my wife but said that would not be necessary. Donna assured her it wouldn't be a problem because her break was coming up and she could use the exercise. Reluctantly, the lady listed the stores she visited, continuing to express her willingness to come back and search the mall herself. My wife asked for her name and phone number and promised to call back within the hour.

Donna took her break and quickly located the lost bags. She called back within the hour to relay the good news. The stressed-out customer was elated, promising to come immediately to pick them up. She arrived two hours later with a brightly colored gift bag containing a freshly-baked loaf of bread and a jar of home-made preserves. With a big smile and many words of appreciation, she told Donna no one had ever extended the type of customer service she just received. She said the gift bag was her thank you for providing great customer service, and furthermore said Donna had earned a life-time customer. She even promised to tell others about her great customer service experience.

When my wife shared this story, I wondered if I would have been willing to do what she had done. I've asked myself many times if, after receiving the phone call, I would simply look around the counter, fail to find the merchandise, return to the phone, say "*I'm sorry,*" and go on about my business. Or would I have gone the extra mile to look for the lost purchases? What would you have done? Would you go to the extra trouble? I've asked thousands of seminar attendees that question – because the answer gives you insight into whether or not you're willing to do what others are not.

My wife's secret to success is her willingness to do what others are not willing to do. She demonstrates this willingness every day with every person she meets. And so it is with you: Just like Donna, you have the choice to go the extra mile or you can choose to sit back and hope something good happens.

The roadmap to new home sales success is within the pages of *Building Results*. To help you adopt the *Success Guarantee* idea, I've highlighted critical concepts from each chapter to serve as a guidepost on your personal journey to success.

When you practice these, you place in motion your own *Success Guarantee*. Never forget that success is defined as being 'willing to do what others are not willing to do'. You have a choice to make – choose the direction Donna takes every day or follow the example of the 29 students who chose not to implement the 'immediate phone call' idea. Choose wisely, because you will become the sum total of your decisions.

Chapter 1
Turning Point

Building Results Selling
Building Results selling is about doing things for people while Critical Path Selling is about doing things to people.

Meeting Customer Needs
New home prospects do not want to be controlled. They first want to look and get a feel for the home before they answer questions

Chapter 2
Communications Principles and New-Home Selling

Bridging the Needs
New-home selling is intelligent conversation between two parties who have a similar goal in mind – the purchase and sale of a new home. This goal is reached only when a salesperson and prospect discover common points of interest that bring about alignment and agreement. These two critical issues require a simple formula before they occur: In order to lead, a salesperson must first be willing to follow.

Balancing the Relationship
Understand that successful new home selling is the result of excellent communication skills, not a critical-path selling process. Understand how people communicate with each other, and learn what communication skills work best in most interpersonal situations.

Six Communication Principles
The critical six Communication Principles follow some of the tenets of NLP rapport building. Each principle shows how to acknowledge the customer's needs at the same time the salesman's needs are met while balancing their selling priorities.

1. You are always communicating.

2. The mind and body are parts of the same system.

3. Ride the horse in the direction it is going.

4. The person with the most knowledge will have the most influence.

5. The map is not the territory.

6. The exception is not the rule.

Rule about Liking

In order for people to like you, you first must like them. Begin today to practice this simple but powerful rule by demonstrating through your physiology, tonality and words that you want to help customers get what is important to them.

Communicating with Yourself

You are what you think about. If you think negatively about your customers, your physical actions will be consistent with your thoughts.

Ride the Horse in the Direction It Is Going

An experienced horse rider knows that a horse resists attempts to control it until it is comfortable with the rider. Any attempt to control the horse before that could end in the rider getting thrown off. In a way your customers demonstrate similar behavior. Initially they don't want to be controlled. They want freedom to explore your homes and community and reach a comfort level consistent with their buying motivations. Any attempt to control them before they're ready could raise their defenses and cause them to move away from you.

The Sales Process

Every successful sale begins with rapport, moves to understanding, then to influence and finally to a sale.

Finding Common Ground

Building Results' teaches you to find common ground aligning you with your customer. Once you've identified with your customer, the next step is to ask questions to discover and understand what his priorities are. When you can demonstrate understanding, your customer will allow you to influence them toward a new home purchase.

Understanding Needs

When you ask discovery and qualifying questions, you're uncovering all the information included in your customer's map. The more you discover about his needs and important issues, the more accurate you'll be in matching them with the right product, features and options.

Participating

Once you ask your discovery questions and have listened carefully to the responses, you're ready to enter the territory (model home and community) with your customer. Your success in being part of his total buying experience requires you to be part of your customer's new map.

Control What You Can – Let Go What You Can Not

Learn to let go of what you can't control and to work with what you can. Keep reminding yourself that most of the people you meet sincerely want your help. Focus on them, give them the best you have, and you'll experience new home sales success.

Chapter 3
Preparation

Relating to the Prospect

Remember to your prospective buyer, you are the builder. You're the person who must inspire confidence, trust and credibility; the one who must reflect honesty, integrity, stability, dependability, caring and professionalism. You're the person who must relate personally to each and every unique prospect.

Builder

Very few buyers really know enough about the homebuilders they're considering to assess their reliability, integrity and commitment to customer satisfaction. It's a fundamental part of your job as salesperson to make the builder stand out positively and professionally from the rest.

Builder Policies

Whether you are an experienced veteran or a rookie, take time to meet with each department head to learn specific policies of that department, knowledge you need to answer customers' questions with confidence and enthusiasm.

Community

Take time to study your community to discover those things that separate your community from the competition. Meet with the person who purchased the land, and find out why he chose this site. Talk to the customers who have purchased; understand how and why they made the decision to purchase.

Area

Many home purchases are made because of the location. It's up to you provide your customer with area information so they can make an informed decision. Place all information into an Area Binder, and set it out where prospects can see and read it.

Product

Product knowledge of homes and options is a must. If you fail to understand your product, you will certainly fail. When you meet prospects for the first time, understand they are there to look at product. They want to compare your product to the competition. If you can't answer their questions, your chance of losing the sale increases greatly.

Homesite

Meet with your community builder or sales manager and walk each homesite asking questions about the value of one over the other. Armed with this information, include the homesite visit into every new home sales presentation.

Financing

Most homebuyers require a loan to purchase a new home. This fact provides you with a unique opportunity to demonstrate knowledge in an area that can be very complicated. Meet with loan officers and ask them to explain the various finance programs to learn positives and negatives of each. Learn which companies specialize in good or A credit, and those that welcome B or C credit. Develop an ongoing relationship, take them to lunch regularly and depend on them to keep you up to date on market changes. Their companies will make far more profit from your buyer than you or your builder; it's certainly in their best interest to help you.

Resistance

No community is perfect. Each has features that are less than desirable, some of which may impact a significant percentage of your prospects. You must identify these features and carefully prepare a strategy for handling resistance before you are face to face with a customer.

Competition

It has been said – and it is true – that the only thing you cannot match is people. A competing builder can match your price, your product and your promotions, but he can't match you. Take time to study the salesperson with whom you are competing. Know his selling strengths and weaknesses. Capitalizing on his weakness may be the difference between success and failure in your community.

Planning

Prepare a plan for each day with a specific time noted for each activity. Set specific priorities for each day, starting with the most important or difficult items. Remember Paretto's 80/20 Rule. 80% of your results are generated by 20% of your activities. Do the critical 20% first! Average performers wallow in the 80% non-critical items and are forever doomed to mediocrity.

Image of Professionalism

It's not enough to offer a fine community and excellent homes. You personally must reflect a professional image. The ways you dress, talk and act are just as important as the housing values you represent.

Sales Center

Is your sales center clean? Is everything orderly and neat? Remember, you are reflected in your environment. You hardly create a sense of confidence and trust if the sales center is not properly refreshed or you're fumbling through stacks of paper or drawers to find things.

Model Homes

Model homes are vitally important to your efforts. Not only do they serve as a showcase for your builder's product, features, and options but they offer the customer a tangible representation of what their new home will be like.

Chapter 4
Connecting

The Connecting Process
Six distinct elements make up the connecting process:

1. Attitude

2. Sales presentation

3. Building rapport

4. Determining needs

5. Understanding the importance of time

6. The greeting

Attitude

You cannot sell new homes with a negative attitude. Homebuyers have their own fears and uncertainties – they do not need yours. One solution is to keep your immediate sales objectives in mind. The builder is properly concerned about long-range objectives, but you must be concerned about making and closing sales now.

Buying Process

Too many sales representatives give in at the first sign of adversity. Be aware that the homebuyer has a buying process just like you have a selling process. And part of his buying process is to eliminate you.

Building Your Strengths

Set up an inventory of your talents and abilities. List those positive attributes you know you have, and then make a decision to strengthen them. True, you should spend some time each day focusing on your weaknesses, but you must direct most of your energy to building on your strengths.

Competent Professional

It's important to communicate concern for your customers' needs. They want to do business with someone who respects them and genuinely cares about their priorities. They also want you to give them a sense of competency.

Sales Presentation

Many sales representatives think of the presentation as little more than a sales pitch; but, in truth, the presentation is far more comprehensive. It encompasses the way you, the builder, the community and the models are presented to potential customers. It's the impression you and your builder project to the public.

Rapport

Rapport signals a relationship exemplified by agreement, alignment or likeness and similarity. If you agree or align verbally or nonverbally with another person or perhaps bear some likeness to that person, you are in a state of rapport.

Pacing

Pacing is a skill that involves meeting your customer where she is right now, reflecting on what you know to be true, or matching some part of her ongoing experience. It involves presenting to another person those aspects of you that are most like hers. When you pace a customer, you are saying, *"I'm like you. You're safe with me. You can trust me."* Pacing breeds familiarity and thus establishes trust and credibility.

Leading

While pacing is doing something similar to the customer's actions; leading is doing something different. The best strategy is to pace first and then lead. Meet your customer where he or she is and then offer other options. The general rule is that if the customer resists your lead, go back to pacing and look for new opportunities to lead after agreement and alignment has been reestablished.

Communication Elements

Study this chart to understand the significance your physiology, tonality and words have on your ability to establish and maintain rapport.

Communication Elements		Percent of Impact on Rapport
Physiology:	Posture, position, gestures	55
Tonality:	Voice tone, pitch, volume, rate, timbre and inflections	38
Words:	Expressions, key words, criteria, slang	7

Modes of Communication

Each person you meet has a dominant or primary mode of communication. When you make initial contact with new customers, they'll probably be thinking in one of three main representational systems: generating visual images, having feelings, or talking and listening. Identifying the pertinent communication mode at any given time is an important key to their pattern of understanding and therefore is an important element of understanding them and helping them understand you.

Minimal Cues

Minimal cues are small movements made by your customer to let you know that something in their experience has changed. Minimal cues happen whether something good or bad has happened to your customer. The cue denotes a change in thinking or attitude. It's your responsibility to notice the change, stop where you are and ask questions to obtain the information you need.

Identifying with People

There are two ways to look at your customers. You can choose to emphasize the differences between you and them. Or you can choose to emphasize the similarities – the things you share. Emphasize the differences and you'll find it hard to establish rapport. But emphasize your commonalities, and resistance and antagonism disappear. With practice, it becomes easy to find you in your customers' good graces and to ally yourself with them. When people identify with each other, they cooperate.

Listening

Listening in new home sales is vitally important. It is the cornerstone of effective communication. Most salespeople are not good listeners because they were never taught this fine art, yet the problems this causes affect every level of the selling process. Listening helps you work more effectively and accurately, assuring the message you receive is the message your customer sends.

Time

Prospective new homebuyers have a definite strategy for maximizing their time. In order to be successful in new home selling today, you must also have a selling strategy to maximize the prospect's time. Your selling strategy begins to form shortly after your greeting with the following question:

"How much time do you have to spend with me, today?"

Time Strategy

A selling strategy goal is to spend time with your prospect. Research conducted by the Sales Institute provides this important fact – for every thirty minutes you spend with a prospective customer, your chance of closing a sale increases by 50%.

The Connecting Process

The connecting process begins before that first face-to-face meeting with your customer. Your builder has devoted considerable energy and financial resources to assure that your customer's first impression is a positive one. Advertising and promotion, graphics and design, model home parks and displays, all are carefully planned and executed to make a favorable impact on the customer. However, in the final analysis, it is you who will parlay the connecting process into a signed contract.

Chapter 5
Discovery and Qualifying

Discovery Questions

When asking discovery questions, you're asking your customers to share important information – facts that will make it easier to decide if what you are offering satisfies their needs or solves problems. In other words, discovery questions tell you which conditions you must satisfy in order to make a sale.

Precise Discovery Questions

Ask precise discovery questions to quickly understand the conditions you must satisfy in order to ask for the sale. When you understand buying conditions, you align yourself with your prospect's needs and wants, and that leads to a sale.

Six Precise Discovery Questions

There are six precise discovery questions. They are:

1. What is important about the new home we will build for you?

2. What is important about the homesite you select for your new home?

3. What is important about the community you select for your new home?

4. What is important about the location you select for your new home?

5. What is important about the financing you select for your new home?

6. What is important about the builder you select for your new home?

Peeling the Onion

Is there anything else? This question is designed to uncover conditions of which your prospect may not be consciously aware but either wants or would like to have. And if you're able to deliver either wants or like-to-haves, you definitely separate yourself from your competition.

Buying Motivations

There are four primary buying motivations: family, convenience, investment and prestige. One or all four of these motivations may be hidden in the prospect's responses.

Transitional Listening

This important factor provides the bridge between your prospect's decision-making conditions and the conditions that make purchasing a new home possible. Transitional listening makes new home selling easy. All you have to do is ask precise discovery questions and listen carefully for conditions included in every customer response.

Qualifying Questions

Ask qualifying questions to discover conditions that limit the prospects' ability to purchase. Qualifying questions provide answers to personal information that your prospects may not want to share until you earn their confidence and trust.

Seventeen Conditions

All the personal information you need to know about a prospect is available to you – the key is to ask precise discovery questions first and then listen for need-to-know transition opportunities.

Here are the 17 conditions:

Decision-making conditions
1. Home
2. Homesite
3. Community
4. Location
5. Financing
6. Builder

Need-to-know conditions
1. Visit motivation
2. Where presently living
3. Own or rent
4. Family or living situation
5. Employment
6. Timing and urgency
7. Shopping experience
8. Price range
9. Income
10. Initial investment
11. Debt

Emotion and Fact
Never forget that people buy on emotion and justify with fact.

Chapter 6
Building Value

Price and Value
When a prospect visits your model home, they are mentally weighing two things – what do I have to pay and what value do I get for my money?

Value
Value is nothing more than a measure of how badly the customer wants something. It is a mental situation. That's why you are able to influence it.

Features
Details of the home's features tell how the product is made, how it's put together and of what it is made. Actually this is how the price originates. It's the accumulation of profit margins, cost of labor, materials, handling, shipping and warehousing – elements that establish a price.

Benefits
Benefits answer the question – what's in it for me?

Adding Value
You can negotiate a little with price but there's a definite limit as to how much. However, there's no limit as to how much value you can add. And adding value is what *Building Value* selling is all about. Features give the customer things to pay for. *Building Value* selling gives the customer reasons to buy. And until your customers have enough reasons to buy – they won't buy.

Chapter 7
Demonstrating the Home

Principles of Demonstrating
There are three principle of demonstrating, they are:

1. Demonstrating is the art of selling features and benefits connected to buying motivations.

2. A good sales presentation doesn't need arguments – it needs demonstrations.

3. You can show more in five minutes than you can tell in one hour.

Seven Reasons to Demonstrate
There are seven reasons to demonstrate the home, they are:

1. To establish your credibility through product knowledge.

2. To sell your company and its reputation for quality construction.

3. To explain included features and sell custom features.

4. To ask any remaining discovery and qualifying questions.

5. To lead prospects to minor decisions by utilizing tie-down and trial-close questions.

6. To sell a trip to the home site, where you and the prospect can look at specific homes or properties.

7. The most compelling reason is simply that people believe what they see.

Demonstration Requirements

Certainly it's important to know how to demonstrate, but knowing what to demonstrate is equally critical, because you might present the wrong thing at the wrong time. In order to know what to demonstrate, you must understand the requirements of an effective presentation. They are: gain a clear understanding of the buyer, organize the demonstration logically, and develop an effective delivery.

Organize the Demonstration

Four elements should be an integral part of every successful demonstration:

1. Customer knowledge

2. Product knowledge

3. Construction knowledge

4. Planning

Demonstrating – A Real Sales Tool

Here's how to make your demonstration a real sales tool: Write out the words ahead of time. Rehearse your demonstration over and over. Let the customer handle the product – involve them and let them demonstrate it to themselves. Tie down each benefit as you demonstrate, thus persuading your customer to agree that each is important.

Option Selling

The selling of options during the demonstration presents a special opportunity to provide additional benefits to everyone involved in the sales process – the customer, the builder and you. Option selling is a positive experience for three reasons:

1. It provides you with a means of tailoring the product to the specific needs of your customer.

2. It enables your customer to customize the home to his exact specifications, thereby 'personalizing' the house and enhancing its desirability.

3. It improves the profitability of your builder.

Art of Demonstrating

The most significant thing to remember about the art of demonstrating is to link features to benefits and then to buying motivations.

Chapter 8
Demonstrating the Homesite

One-of-a-Kind

Second only to the home, its construction, quality and design is the homesite. You won't close many customers if you're unable or unwilling to demonstrate the site. To enhance your homesite selling ability, keep these fundamental principles in mind:

1. Every homesite is unique.

2. Every homesite is different.

3. No two are alike.

Unique Selling Proposition

Every worthy product embodies a unique characteristic, a special quality that makes it desirable. Discover that quality and you define the product's Unique Selling Point.

Matching Home to Homesite

The decision to build a certain home on a particular homesite is made by the production and land department in a carefully considered decision involving many factors – drainage, easements, codes, aesthetic considerations and profitability. These are factors you should understand so you can frame intelligent responses to your customers' questions. The important fact is each homesite will take only a certain type of house.

Planning
Study your homesite list and select your key lots. Decide which homesites represent the best value and which ones you would most like to sell today.

Selection
Select at least two homesites for each home you have to sell. Determine possible reasons for choosing one over the other in terms of benefits offered.

Comparison
If you have two homesites available for the same style, select the two least similar in benefits. Then, when you begin the selection process with the customer, begin with the less likely of the two. If they like it and buy it, you'll still have the one with more benefits available for the next customer.

Narrow the Choice
Don't give your customer too many choices. A buyer can't select from ten properties any more than he can from one hundred. You must narrow the choice down to one or two as quickly as possible.

Homesite Visit
You simply will not sell houses unless you get buyers out of the models and onto the homesites. Push as hard as you can without becoming overbearing. Otherwise, there's a good chance your competitor down the road will get a grip on them and never let go.

Move Them In
When you demonstrate homesites, do it with a dash of flair and imagination. What you want to do is to place the home on the homesite in your customers' imaginations. You want to 'move them in' by creating a finished home in their minds. Use your physiology, tonality and well-chosen words to create a home they can visualize as their own. Putting customers on the right homesite is one of the best services you can provide.

Props
To demonstrate homesites effectively and efficiently, you'll need to acquire a few props. Keep them in the trunk of your car so that they're always readily available to you.

1. 4 pairs of boots

2. 2 umbrellas

3. 4 rain parkas

4. 4 stakes

5. Ball of heavy twine

6. 100-foot measuring tape

7. Plat map

8. Product binder

9. Sold signs

10. Digital camera

Participation
The name of the game is participation, both physical and emotional. Use your imagination to complete that mental image. The more customers are involved with the homesite, the more they imagine themselves living there, and the easier it will be to close.

Separating Yourself from the Competition
If you want to separate yourself from the competition, learn the art of demonstration. Tom Richey is quoted as saying, *"Get your customers to the homesite and you will write"*. Too many salespeople fail to earn their customer's business because they eliminate this important step in the selling process.

Chapter 9
Handling Resistance

Welcome Resistance

There is one consistent in new home sales – homebuyer resistance. In fact, if you don't experience homebuyer resistance, more than likely you won't get the sale.

Misunderstandings and Drawbacks

Homebuyer resistance generally falls into two categories: misunderstandings and drawbacks. Misunderstanding is usually the result of a customer lacking information or being misinformed about a particular feature or benefit. Drawback is usually the result of the product's failure to provide a benefit important to the customer or the customer simply not liking something about your homes.

Four Possibilities

When you first hear a comment that sounds like resistance, remember that it may not be resistance at all. There are at least four other possibilities:

1. A mere comment with no real significance.

2. A request for additional information – misunderstanding.

3. A buying signal that indicates mounting interest.

4. A real problem which must be resolved at the right time – a drawback.

Six-Step Process

While there's no instant formula for making you an expert on *Handling Resistance*, there is a six-step process that will align you with your customer so a good decision can be made.

The six steps are as follows:

1. Agree

2. Pause

3. Question

4. Verify

5. Reframe

6. Tie down

Agree

The purpose of the agreement is to demonstrate to the customer that you are listening and are aware of the resistance. The agreement is designed to give you time to think about how you are going to respond. In reality, it is a stall.

Pause

Do not say or add anything to your agreement. Be quiet. Allow your customer time to mentally process that you are agreeing, not defending or arguing. In some instances a customer's resistance may melt away because nothing can be done about the objection. It is what it is.

Question

Is the resistance simply a misunderstanding or something more serious, such as a drawback? You can't overcome resistance until you know what it is. Go beyond the words and be sure you understand what's keeping your customer from making a decision.

Verify

The four primary motivations for purchasing are convenience, family, investment and prestige. Verifying requires that you listen very carefully for evidence of these emotions. If you hear a misunderstanding or drawback with one of these emotions, verify it to demonstrate understanding.

Reframing

Reframing provides your customer with a new point of view – a different way to think about or look at a misunderstanding or a drawback. Until your customers consider alternative views, you're facing a losing battle. When customers begin to look at their objection from a different perspective, they're changing the way they think and understand – or reframing. There are five reframes: minimize, convert to a positive, third-party testimonial, documentation and pro and con.

Tie Down

The tie down requires your customer to respond to your reframe. His response tells you whether he accepted or declined your reframe. If you don't get a positive response, relax, take a deep breath and mentally consider your next reframe. Remember there are five possible reframes. What you may have discovered is that you are dealing with hard resistance – a serious drawback.

Questions and Resistance

Remember customers are filled with questions about things that interest them. The point is not to avoid or fear questions and resistance, but to welcome both. When you answer your customer's misunderstandings or drawbacks, it gives them the confidence that they are making the correct decisions when they say "*Yes.*"

Chapter 10
Closing

Asking for the Order

If you don't ask for the order, chances are you won't make the sale. That's the essential truth of the new home selling profession, because when you ask for an order you provide the motivation your customer needs to take action.

Rules of the Game

The following general statements best summarize the fundamentals of closing – the rules of the game:

1. Lead people to minor decisions

2. Understand how people buy

3. Assume success

4. Close constantly

5. Create urgency

6. Maintain control

Minor Decisions

The more your customer says yes, the harder it will be to say no. Persuade them to agree that your homes satisfy their requirements. Ask affirmative questions or tie-downs throughout your sales presentation and especially during discovery.

How People Buy

For most people a home represents the largest single investment of their lifetime. The ultimate decision whether or not to buy is made by balancing benefits against disadvantages. In order to close, benefits must outweigh disadvantages. The buyer must have complete confidence that owning your home has more benefits than any other home he's considering.

Assuming the Sale

Personal confidence is one of the most important keys to successful closing. When you assume that the sale has been made, it makes the buying decision seem smaller and less painful. The bigger a decision, the more anxious and indecisive your prospects become. If you communicate this assumption, prospects feel they are not making a new decision; they're just going along with a decision already made.

Solution Provider

When you begin to see yourself as a solution provider and not a salesperson, the closer you become to earning the right to ask for the sale.

Close Early and Often

If you do not close early and often, you run the risk of losing your customer's respect. Customers know why you are there – they expect you to close – they even expect you to close many times. If you do not close repeatedly, they will intuitively perceive you as weak and unprofessional.

Creating Urgency

Urgency is a function of time and personal motivations. What is urgent to one prospect may not be to another. For example, some people place little value on money, while others will jump to close if they learn that a price increase is imminent. Not everyone will react the same way to your prompts to stimulate urgency, so it's good to develop a range of 'urgent messages'.

Controlling the Sales Environment

To close effectively, you must have control. Ultimately, your conversion of closed sales to available opportunities will depend on how effectively you control the sales environment. The more you learn the art of controlling your sales environment, the easier it will be to help prospects make favorable buying decisions.

Partial Closes

If you are successful in any one of the following categories you should consider each a close:

1. Contract

2. Deposit

3. Appointment

4. Phone call

Chapter 11
Follow Through

First Visit

One thing you can count on in new home sales is that few prospects buy on the first visit. Research studies on the attitudes and actions of new home buyers tell us the following:

1. They typically inspect six to ten new communities or other alternatives before deciding upon a purchase.

2. They typically narrow their interest to three or four new and used homes. This is their short list, homes and builders about which

they are serious. Clearly your objective is to make the short list.
Once they've focused on four or fewer, they're ready for closing.

3. Buyers typically return two to four times to each home they're
    considering before purchasing, unless they've had a lot of product
    exposure or are pressed by urgency, such as relocation.

4. They typically spend four to six hours with a salesperson before
    the close.

Four Steps

The follow through, contrary to what the name may seem to imply, is not limited
to what you do after you say "*Goodbye*". More properly, it could be described as what
you do after you say "*Hello*" and detect that your prospect wants to say "*Goodbye*".
Most new home experts agree four steps lead to an effective follow through. Each step is
dependent upon the successful completion of the step before it. The steps are as follows:

1. Think about your follow through.

2. Justify your follow through.

3. Implement your follow through.

4. Follow up your follow through.

Think Follow Through

A sure-fire way to increase your sales is to think in terms of setting up your
follow through during your initial sales presentation. This means you must watch during
the very first visit for tell-tale signs that they aren't quite ready to buy. Once you receive
these signals, it's time to start thinking about your follow through.

Justify Follow Through

Justify your follow through by laying the groundwork during the prospect's first
visit that initiates a second visit. It's far better to take an action during your initial
interview that provides you with a good reason for setting a future appointment. Then
your phone call will be expected and well received.

Implement Follow Through

Once you've thought about and justified your follow through, the next important step is to implement your strategy – follow through on the action you promised in your justification. That's where the telephone or e-mail comes in handy.

Follow Up Your Follow Through

Following up your follow through means finding new reasons to contact your prospects. It means staying in touch. Successful salespeople never say die. Once they get a customer, they stay in regular contact until the customer either buys or makes another choice.

Full-Time Job

Following through is a full-time job, day in and day out requiring the total application of thought, word and deed. You must constantly think about and justify your follow through. You must always, without fail, implement your follow through, and you must persistently follow up on your follow through.

Some Final Thoughts

Building Results has provided you with a roadmap to follow. Have you started on your journey or are you waiting for just the right moment? If you have started, congratulations, you're on your way to new home sales success. If you haven't, please consider the following story about Tom Watson, the 1982 U.S. Open Champion.

When Jack Nicklaus finished a 4-under par 284, Tom Watson was just stepping to the tee at the par-3 17th hole at Pebble Beach. The distance was 209 yards, with the hole location cut on the left side toward the rear of the green. Watson chose a 2-iron and pulled the shot into the thick rough beside the green.

To make matters worse, he was 20 feet from the hole with no room to work. Using his sand wedge, he sliced a perfect-stroke across the ball and broke into a dance as the ball disappeared into the hole. He followed with another birdie on 18 to win the 1982 U S Open by two strokes. As he was walking off the green to celebrate with family and friends, an announcer stopped him and said, *"Tom, that was sure a lucky a shot on 17."* Tom smiled and said, *"Yes, it* was *a lucky shot; but you know the more I practice, the luckier I get."*

And so it can be with you. Begin today to put into practice all the ideas included in *Building Results,* and you'll be amazed at how 'lucky' you become.

   With regards to luck, just remember that luck can be defined as preparation meeting opportunity. In new home selling, you meet opportunity every day in the form of new customers. The real question is 'are you prepared'? Start today by preparing for the successful future you deserve – one that begins when you make the commitment – to do what others are not willing to do.

   Good luck and good selling!

Building Results for the Housing Industry

Workshops and Training
by Robert E. Hafer & Associates

Robert E. Hafer & Associates provides a revolutionary program of teaching, coaching, and consulting to the new home industry. Precisely tailored for builders, new home sales professionals and Realtors, these programs are well known for jump-starting sales professionals' careers and entire companies' sales turn-arounds.

Building Results challenges traditional sales principles with a combination of traditional critical path processes, Neuro-Linguistics Programming and dynamic communications techniques from some of the business world's most successful programs. The final almost magical ingredient involves leading and following – in a genius combination that literally blows the lid off conventional sales techniques.

No one has ever successfully combined these powerful ingredients into one cohesive, comprehensive roadmap to success. Building Results' workshops is designed for salespeople who are willing to think differently, act on their new thoughts consistently and *do what others are not willing to do.* For them, the outcome is guaranteed – new home selling success far beyond the expected.

Even more fascinating, these wonderful possibilities and ideas not only will dramatically change your selling career but also your personal interaction with family, friends, customers and business acquaintances.

For information on *Building Results* workshops and consulting services, contact:

Bob Hafer, Robert E. Hafer & Associates LLC
4361 Mill Creek Road, Dallas, Texas 75244
(972) 795-5926 • buildingresults@BobHafer.com